My North Dakota Prairie Childhood

The background history and story of a
North Dakota child growing up in a
Lutheran parsonage during the Great Depression.

By Rose Marie Brauer

May 15, 1995

To Anita and Fred —
You are terrific hosts,
and I enjoyed every minute
of my weekend of the 40th
Anniversary of Christ
Lutheran Church.
Thanks and God's peace,
Love,
Rose Marie

Published by Gregory Publishers
4425 Crestland Drive
St. Louis, Missouri 63121
Phone: (314) 389-8054

May   1990: First Edition, First Printing
August 1990: Second Printing
March   1991: Third Printing
June   1993: Fourth Printing
August 1994: Fifth Printing

ISBN: 0-9643204-0-1 $15.00

Library of Congress Catalog Card Number 94-79031

Acknowledgments

To my husband, Donald Brauer, whose silent encouragement, time and patience in typing the family tree, and friendship over five decades gave me the desire to put my thoughts and feelings on paper.

To my son Dr. Gregory Oetting, whose life and example give me motivation to do what seems the impossible;

To my constant friend, Lori Duesenberg, whose loving kindness has continuously encouraged me to write this book;

To my family who has given personal input, who love me just as I am, and who shared my childhood on the prairie;

My North Dakota relatives and friends, who gave me motivation and information;

And to Lynnda Cramer, whose uncanny ability to read my writing and understand my feelings and make reasonable sentences, has made the dream of this book a reality.

This book is dedicated to my dear parents, Walter Edwin Leininger and Helen Rose Behrmann Leininger, with deepest love and thanks for their steadfast support and complete faith in me in my pursuit of goals; for the gift of life and my most joyous country childhood.

June, 1990

Contents

Prologue . . . . Page 11

Chapter One . . . . Page 13
    "Oh Give Me Land, Lots'a Land"

Chapter Two . . . . Page 27
    "Oh Give Me a Home, Where the Buffalo Roam"

Chapter Three . . . . Page 45
    "Oh Beautiful for Spacious Skies, for Amber Waves of Grain"

Chapter Four . . . . Page 57
    "Let It Snow, Let It Snow, Let It Snow"

Chapter Five . . . . Page 69
    "The More We Get Together, Together, Together..."

Chapter Six . . . . Page 77
    "Those Jolly Old Blues"

Chapter Seven . . . . Page 85
    "'Readin' and 'Ritin and 'Rithmetic..."

Chapter Eight . . . . Page 97
    "I Wanna Grow Up!"

Chapter Nine . . . . Page 113
    "Night and Day, You Are the One..."

Epilogue . . . . Page 129

Family Trees . . . . Page 133

To everything there is a season,
and a time to every purpose under the heaven:
A time to be born, a time to die;
a time to plant, and a time to pluck up that which is planted;
A time to kill, and a time to heal;
a time to break down, and a time to built up;
A time to weep, and a time to laugh;
a time to mourn, a time to dance;
A time to cast away stones, and a time to gather stones together;
a time to embrace, and a time to refrain from embracing;
A time to get, and a time to lose;
a time to keep and a time to cast away;
A time to rend, and a time to sew;
a time to keep silence, and a time to speak;
A time to love, and a time to hate;
a time of war and a time of peace...

Ecclesiastes 3 : 1-8

Prologue

Friends and family have often said to me for years, "Why don't you write down your thoughts and feelings about your past and write a book?" Well, that is exactly what I did. The only negative thought I had was that I'd probably never actually complete a book. How could I ever tell about my past?

After my son, Gregory, completed medical school, got married, and moved to Richmond, Virginia (for seven years of residency), it left a great void in my life, a much too familiar feeling. I needed to fill this void with the happier days of my youth, to get more acquainted with my true self and my past; to release those feelings, whether they were joyful or sad. This was the real motivation to write this book.

I wrote this volume not only for those with loneliness and losses in their lives, but for the many farmers and their families who still experience the eternal frustrations of weather and "making ends meet" - to let them know we understand and care.

For the pastor's families whose lives continue to be lived "in a fishbowl" - you can make it as a "P.K." and become normal acceptable human beings.

My purpose is also to give some highlights of North Dakota history and to educate the city folks on the true life and love of living on the plains.

Chapter One

"Oh Give Me Land, Lots of Land,
Under the Starry Skies Above...."

I can pinpoint the exact moment when I knew I had to write this book. It was in the darkest hours of a rainy March morning back in 1989 - at three a.m., to be exact. I don't remember what I was dreaming, but somehow I sat bolt upright in bed, "possessed", as they say. I got up and went directly to the kitchen where I began to write down absolutely <u>everything</u> that came to mind. Like North Dakota sunsets (I can remember each one I loved), red winged blackbirds dipping over fields of new cut wheat, the high note of a meadow lark (the state bird), wild rambling roses (the state flower) lacing miles of fence line, winter-white fields stitched tight by the barbed lines of bare shelter belt branches... And dressing in Dad's study where the wood stove burned the hottest, or sledding off haystacks, and shocking wheat on long summer afternoons or washing our clothes in the new wringer machine on the back porch, and long Sundays of Daddy's voice over worshipful heads...

By dawn I'd covered more than a dozen pages of notebook paper on both sides with my tiny scrawl; and I'd only just started. There is so much more to tell and I feel I have to "tell my love" - or waste into a void; for I've loved my North Dakota homeland...it is still, to this day, "my love." But who would care? How dare I proclaim myself worthy of a story no one would give a hoot about? Millions of women have lead lives more interesting than mine. When I used to tell my young sons what it was like to live in a prairie farm town in the Depression, they'd roll their eyes and groan: "Aw, MMMooommmm!" Ancient history.

But I can't shake myself free of it, this need to tell of a life and land so rich and yielding. I suppose everyone has a certain "place" in life, a certain landscape real or remembered that makes you feel the most alive and happy; a place you can always go to in your mind, to find strength and solace; a place so familiar to you that you can touch its surfaces and seasons, you know them so well, and thrill to the particular crystalline glare of a noon time sun on fresh, young snow, or stand breathless in the midnight moon's quiet brilliance. The image I always see, when I call it up, is of newly harrowed fields in spring when the earth, deep black and clean and fertile, renders itself so frankly and willingly to the till, so eagerly to the seed. I grew up in all that bright young power of growth and harvest; and I know that I would never have been able to deal with the blows fate has dealt me without knowing that those fields, those prairies and all that midnight sky bright with endless stars - it has always been there for me, a strength ever ready. And I want my story to be that too, for my sons and their young children coming along, a presence, a resource, always there, always true. So I begin my story as bright and eager as a shiny gold star atop a bushy pine tree - I was born December 12, 1931.

But I'm getting a little bit ahead of myself. First of all I must tell you that I was extremely blessed to have two good parents. My father, Walter Edwin Leininger, was born in Boone, Iowa, fifth son and last child of a farmer who came with three of his eight children up to North Dakota where he bought three sections of land (a vast amount by today's standards). We don't know much about the Leininger line except that they hailed from the Leiningen Valley in Alsace-Lorraine, a rich, fertile (and much fought over) province between Germany and France. I imagine that the broad and untouched plains of the Dakotas captured their fancy - perhaps reminded them of the place their ancestors left in the old world.

My father was the only son to become a preacher; he spent his life serving in the Lutheran church. It was common in those days for younger sons to go into the ministry. And so too, at least one daughter ended up marrying a pastor, or a missionary in some far off place. My Dad's two brothers John and Michael married sisters of this missionary, and their descendants still live in the same area around Binford, North Dakota, as do many of their descendants to this very day - but I'll tell some more about them later.

Dad was only fourteen when his father died - too young, I think, to make the promise his mother exacted of him when the family (only one or two children still at home then) left the farm and moved to St. Paul, Minnesota in 1911. (Albert, an older brother was working there.) She asked Dad to become a Lutheran pastor, and promising he would, promptly enrolled in Concordia College where he began classes in the adjoining high school, called a "prep school," in preparation for a life in the Lutheran ministry. My sisters agree with me in the feeling that he did enjoy his work to a certain extent, but that his heart was really elsewhere. He was very talented with things mechanical, and loved the outdoors, especially the wilder aspects of nature - which is probably why he so loved his years in Canada. He studied hard for the ministry despite many doubts - but did honor her wish to the end of his life. But I think he always wondered "what might have been" had he chosen otherwise. I will add here that when he retired, he and Mother moved back to St. Paul where he continued to visit the sick and elderly in hospitals and nursing homes, from 1968 to 1981, when they moved in with me here in St. Louis due to his deteriorating health.

He met my mother, Helen Rose Behrmann, while he was serving as a vicar and teacher in a Lutheran parish and school in Indianapolis, Indiana. Dad was just about ten years older than Mother when he came there; I think he taught her in one of his classes for a time. At any rate, while Mother was developing a mild school girl crush on him, <u>he</u> was falling in love with her middle sister, Inez.

But tragedy struck them all not long after he left to finish his seminary training. The Behrmanns lived just outside the Indianapolis city limits, where they worked their strawberry farm. One morning the three girls were waiting for the city bus, which stopped just across the street from their home. The bus stopped and the girls started to cross the street. In the meantime, a neighbor and friend had stopped behind the bus, and called to them that she would gladly pick them up. Stella and my mother heard her call and walked behind the bus to the car. Apparently Inez didn't hear the call and ran in front of the bus to get on it. The bus driver must not have seen her - and drove right over her. The two sisters stood in horror as they watched their sister go down beneath the front wheel. They ran screaming and crying down the lane home to get their parents. Their father came running and picked Inez up, carried her into the house and frantically called for police and ambulance. But she was dead. She was only eighteen, and the family mourned her death terribly, especially my mother. In fact, I don't think she's ever gotten over it. Dealing with it is too painful, so she carries that dull ache around in her heart; an ache that was compounded many times in the next fifty years, an ache that lives there still.

This is a good place to stop and look at Mother's life from the perspective of years and happenings, for they were crucial not only to her but to us as well. Raised to be a relatively genteel young lady of modest means in a thriving midwestern city, she developed certain ideals and expectations of life, and deep attachments to her family and roots. She loved both her sisters, and was to lose them both within a ten year period of her own life which was very intense and unhappy. Her sister Stella, who was four years older, died during the birth of her second child (not uncommon in those days when childbirth was often life threatening.) Mother was pregnant with Lois (in 1930), and was unable to make the trip to Indianapolis; because it was summer, the family needed to bury her right away. Stella's two children, Inez and Norman, were cared for by my grandmother Behrmann until she died seven years later of a stroke and grief. Tanta (Aunt) Rose, an older maiden lady who stayed with my Behrmann grandparents, took care of them after that. She lived to an old age, and never married.

As I mentioned, my mother's mother died seven years after Stella's death at the age of fifty-eight of a stroke; so that by the time Mother was only thirty-seven, she had literally no immediate family left. Consider too her deep loneliness and the difficult and demanding role as a preacher's wife. Like all preachers' wives, she had to present the image of perfection and propriety in almost every aspect of her life. No wonder her smiles were rare, her laughter precious.

Now, of course, a trained health professional, I can understand her grief and subsequent behavior, and tolerate it better. Her life is a sad testimony to the price of poor self esteem, aborted dreams and endless sacrifice. A widow now, she lives in high rise apartments for seniors near my sister Dorothy and her pastor husband Wally, in Yakima, Washington. How sad that only now, with the wisdom of hindsight, can we children give love and comfort to one whose frustrated torment and iron will so angered us all at times. We try - and hope it's not too late.

But let us back up about sixty-five years! Mother's love for Inez and her subsequent grief took a cruel twist as time passed. After my father had finished his seminary training and graduated in 1923, he got his first call in the small town of Frobisher in Saskatchewan, Canada. He lived as a bachelor there, and apparently kept up a fairly frequent five year correspondence with Mother and her family. When he'd finished his time in Frobisher, he came back to Indianapolis and rekindled whatever sparks were still there from his lost love, Inez. I'm not sure what Mother made of this, and she had right to wonder. Did Walter really like her? Love her? Or was he thinking of Inez when he wrote and talked to her? Certainly his grief for Inez played a part here; the Behrmanns felt his loss of a sweetheart, just as they felt the loss of a daughter and sister. Did Mother ever love Dad? Could he, in fact, ever recover from Inez's death enough to love any woman as she deserved? So many unanswered questions, especially for Mother, then a young woman who would need a husband in a time when women either married or faced a spinster's lonely life.

I'm pretty sure that Mother never felt toward my father all the passion she wanted to think was possible. And I'm pretty sure my father was smart enough to realize he could not give Mother the real love she deserved. Remember too, that the possibilities of finding someone you could get along with were especially slim for women in those days, because there simply were no other options. You either married somebody, or you taught school and cared for older relatives until you died a lonely maiden aunt. But the facts of dating and marriage in their time and place were hard and few. A man and woman did well to find someone compatible, marry, then work and raise a family. This was especially true for people of the farming background from which my father came. Prairie life allowed no time for romance. And therein lies the rub; Mother was not prepared for prairie life.

My mother came from a very genteel home, and she was proud of a superior intelligence. She often showed us kids her report cards - all straight As, and some A+s!! After graduation from high school, she found a very good job as a bookkeeper with the Mayer Company in Indianapolis, a job she really loved. She had been exposed to the nice things of life, and she saved her money for the niceties she wanted in her home - beautiful china, fine linens, all stored away in her hope chest. And where would her chosen husband take her? I'm sure she knew where he wanted to settle - but I don't think she had any idea about the realities of life in the wilds. There were no National Geographic TV documentaries for her enlightenment on the subject of the Canadian frontier. Perhaps she really did think it would all be a romantic adventure.

Then too, perhaps Walter Leininger's offer was as good as she could hope for. How could you go wrong marrying a man of the cloth? And besides, he had given her a ring - and a ring was tantamount to marriage. A ring on your finger and you were married. She's admitted lately, she really didn't want to marry him, but didn't want to disappoint him; she felt pressured into it.

So there was nothing else to do but marry the man, which she did in 1927, and have his babies. It was just a matter of business, really, and whether it was or wasn't the will of God (which all God fearing folk believed it was) didn't really figure into it. And of course there was no such thing as birth control then, or none that they knew of. When you married, you just had babies, and most women had at least five or six; many had more. Well, what was there to do about it? You washed clothes on a wash board, you hung wet clothes up to freeze on the line outside; after a few hours, while they were still wet, you broke them off to carry inside, where they were hung again in the basement or kitchen on clothes racks. Then you ironed them, and each sweep of the iron, each meal of the day, each wipe of the towel, just sealed you further into a life you couldn't change. Perhaps that explains Mother's "escape" in later years (after Dad had retired), to a job as a sales clerk in a St. Paul, Minnesota clothing store. She loved the work, though Dad was very much against it. She worked there five years until a heart attack ended her escape.

I have a nice studio portrait photograph of my mother taken at about the time she married my father. She had the short, standard cold waved hairdo called the "Marcel", popular in the twenties; and the grave resignation in her eyes that was never to lighten. She was pretty, in her way; as pretty as you could expect a woman to be on the prairies. In her new life in Canada, my mother was known as the "Frau Pastorin", the highly esteemed position of the wife of the pastor in those small, hardy German and Russian settlements. It's taken years for me to realize what she must have gone through to have all that veneration heaped upon her when she secretly struggled to maintain the act she lived everyday as the loving and dutiful wife and mother. My love and appreciation for her and her valiant fulfilling of a very difficult role have increased over the years. I see now that she never had her own identity, and never had the time or opportunity to find it. She was always the pastor's wife, the pastor's five children's mother, the congregation's maternal solace at the pastor's side. But what else was she? Perhaps she never found out. At any rate, I don't think she was really happy - ever, in her entire life there, perhaps anywhere.

Anyway, Walter and Helen married and left immediately for Dad's next post in Oxbow, Saskatchewan. I must add here that Dad was often in charge of several small posts of German and Russian immigrants. This meant he often made trips to other even smaller settlements, over a large area of land. Vacancies in the Lutheran church were frequent, especially in the frozen wastes of Canada. My mother, who was about 21 or so, left behind running water, indoor toilets, electricity, even neighbors, for the Wilds of the Great North and the Will of God.

Poor Mother; she had three babies in the first three years of her marriage. Dorothy was born in Oxbow in 1929. In 1930 Lois was born in Indianapolis. Dad took a parish in McNutt in 1931 where I was born in December. Mom was literally pregnant non-stop for three years. At this time she was twenty five and Dad was thirty four. Bob was also born in McNutt in spring of 1933. There was a lapse of four years when Estelle (for some reason always known as "Tudy") came along in 1937.

As you may guess by now, taking Mother to Oxbow, Canada, was like placing a hothouse flower in a meat locker. Mother hated it from the very first and let my father know in those subtleties of communication only desperate women have - and they all spelled "GUILT" for Dad. An example: she used to tell us that in those first weeks in the Oxbow cabin, Dad had left her for some days on a hunting trip. She said she was so lonely she sat down and wrote seven long letters without stopping. He probably realized he'd made a mistake in bringing this young city girl to a one room "cabin" (really just a deer blind closed in) in the wilderness. No central heating, no indoor plumbing, no electricity!! He had loved his single years up there, loved the excitement and the challenge of the elements, the thrill of hunting and fishing. Many have been the times we children have remarked that Dad should have remained a bachelor in the Yukon and Mother a city school teacher, even if a single one.

By the time Mother was pregnant with Lois, Dad was having stomach problems which became serious enough for him to seek medical attention. Mother, of course, was only too ready to leave, so they agreed to go back to

Indianapolis where they stayed with her parents, and stored their belongings in a trailer parked not far from the house. Dad's stomach problems were never accurately diagnosed at that time, but the mysterious stomach pains faded, and everybody's mood improved, especially after Lois was born in 1930. But Dad felt again drawn to Canada, and, willing to try once more, Mother returned with him and two and a half babies (!), this time to McNutt (this time to a real house), where I was born in 1931.

When Mother was pregnant with me, both she and Dad had talked a lot about this one being a boy. I think they were a little bit desperate for one; the boy would carry on the name, he would get the best education in a good college, he would be the one who would be somebody.

So naturally, my birth was a disappointment at first; but then Mother seemed to have cheered up some, and named me "Rose Marie" because part of that was her own name, and too, she'd seen an operetta by that title (probably back in Indianapolis when Lois was born) and had fallen in love with the name. I think she might have been even a little proud of it, because no one was allowed to shorten it one bit. It was always "Rose Marie", and both she and Dad let everyone know that death would befall any who would dare to shorten it to Rose, or Rosie. (For which I am grateful!) Dad knew I was a serious tomboy from the very first and called me "Wee Wee" out of affection. My sisters to this day think Dad favored me, at least that's what they say.

I chose to arrive on the very cold night of December 12, 1931, in McNutt of Canada's Saskatchewan province (about 40 miles north of the North Dakota border.) Mother tells me it was about 20 degrees below zero that night when they sent for the doctor. She'd just finished ordering some Christmas things from the Eaton's catalogue. I was born at home because all babies in that time and place were; if the doctor got there in time (his average call involved about a twenty mile car trip), fine, but often as not, he didn't. Well, this time he came in time (they'd called for him at 1 a.m.) but didn't really do anything much; just played cards with Dad until I showed up around 3 a.m., weighing in at six and one half pounds.

At least McNutt offered Mother a decent house to live in. By the time I'd arrived, we had a square, white frame house, one story; a makeshift second story of two rooms for the three girls was begun later. I don't think it was ever finished. Actually, all our houses looked somewhat alike as we moved from parish to parish. Being a preacher family, we usually lived in a sort of compound which included house, barn, buggy shed, cemetery and church. The houses were

21

usually (except for Oxbow) roomy two story square frame places painted white. In fact, I don't remember even seeing houses painted anything other than white - unless it was grey, which usually meant the paint was cheap. And I think too, that we had a porch swing on every house. There is nothing quite so relaxing on a hot summer afternoon and evening, than to lie back on it's wide seat and swing slowly...back...forth...until time for supper.

But back to McNutt. I'm told that not long after my birth, Mother developed pleurisy, a painful lung infection that grips the ribs with an almost electric force with every breath. Though she was bed ridden for a time, Dad still would have to prop her up so she could breathe when the pain was bad. He also gave her shots of whiskey, which I doubt the doctor knew about; Dad was a great believer in a shot of whiskey now and then, when medicinal occasions demanded it. Difficult as life was in McNutt, it was the birth place of the much longed for Boy Child!! Brother Robert (Bob to us) arrived in 1933, with much excitement; now the family was complete.

But when Dad again began to feel poorly and doses of whiskey failed to help, my parents decided to leave McNutt and go again to Indianapolis, this time to see a specialist. So we all packed up and moved to my mother's home city, and lived with her parents for the duration of the time it took for the doctors to deal with Dad's mysterious symptoms. (Actually it would be another ten years before they could diagnose diabetes. Today, it's obvious his pains were due to stress, but back then - "stress" hadn't been invented yet!) Again the family stabilized in the environment Mother so craved, marred only by one sad incident. Once when the family was away from their place, thieves broke into the trailer and dragged Mother's large trunk into a nearby field. It was full of her most treasured things, linens and the like. All of them were taken, the trunk left in the field, its drawers all pulled out. Dorothy says she can still see that picture vividly in her mind...it seemed so utterly cruel to Mother, to whom those lovely things meant so much.

After a time though, Dad felt well enough to try a different profession - farming. Even though he was the youngest child and promised to the ministry, he'd still inherited some land in North Dakota from his father, who had died years before. His brothers and numerous extended family had been farming their land for two or three generations now up in Binford, North Dakota, so why not join them? He had farming in his blood; he was a Leininger, after all. So we moved up to Binford in 1933, when Dad unofficially left the ministry of the Lord for that of the Land.

I'm sure my father was delighted to return to an area so densely populated with his own kin; Mother, I'm sure, was not; but she was willing to give American farm life a try. When they heard we were coming, Dad's brothers John and Michael and various cousins and relatives, got to work and built us a house on Dad's land next to John's farm. We lived in a granary until the house was habitable. This was the only time we really lived on a "farm", and I qualify that by saying we lived on Dad's inherited farm land, and he worked on John's and Michael's farms during these five years.

During this time on the farm is when Grandma Behrmann, Mom's mother, died in Indianapolis. It was in the dead of winter when Dad took us by sleigh ride to the train, my very first train ride which I can faintly remember. Bob and I went with Mom as we were not yet of school age. Mom was very pregnant – Tudy was ready to be born, but Mom had to bury her mother first – Tudy came the day after. Mother said the doctor gave her some castor oil and it wasn't too long after that when labor ensued and Tudy was born – it was her fifth and last child.

John and Michael deserve a little explanation since they were so much a part of my childhood, and their children, now in their seventies and eighties, are still alive and active on their North Dakota family farms to this day. These children take over their grandparents' acres, some even live in the same square farm houses they knew as kids. John and his wife Ida had five children, the liveliest of whom are Kenneth and his wife Hazel, in their seventies, who had four children and still live on the prairie homeplace with their son John and his wife Linda. Uncle John and Aunt Ida's place, now Ken's and Hazel's, has always been there for us - always there, unchanging. John was an older brother, Dad the youngest, and because we lived near them in Binford, they helped each other out a lot, Dad being large and rangy, and John small and thin. Uncle Mike, the oldest brother, and Aunt Clara had eight children, the most notable of whom is daughter Alice, who at eighty-plus lives with her husband Bill on the farm with four of their sons (they had twelve children), all bachelors in their forties and fifties. She calls them "The Boys." Alice writes long, effusive letters about their life on the farm and what each of her hundreds of kinfolk are doing. I've enclosed a "short" letter here, written at Christmas time a few years ago. Alice loves to write letters, though I suspect she is probably putting up strawberry jam at this very minute. But at any rate, here's Alice:

December 15, 1985
Dear Rose Marie and Don,
    Just getting a good start on my Christmas letters, and Christmas is almost here. Seems like it comes earlier every year, or it maybe I'm slowing down. Will be eighty on

December 28, and Bill will be eighty-nine this January 2. If we make it 'til then. He has had a sore left leg and foot again, but it is almost back to normal now. He hasn't been doing his chicken chores for a long time now, since he's been feeling better (we had snow), and he never got started again. Tim does chicken chores mornings, and I do them about 5 p.m. I like to do them if the boys keep the snow out of the way, which they usually do. I can't walk in snow, I have a bad leg. Can't tell for sure what the problem is, as it jumps around from hip to knee to ankle. If I sit at the sewing machine too long patching overalls it really hurts. But a good rub with Ben-Gay and it's OK. Now what do you think this is?

Had so many eggs on hand - was wondering who we could give some to, and all at once we'd sold seventy dozen in December. That's good; we only charge sixty cents.

The boys keep busy too. They have a hundred and fifty head of cattle and fifty to sixty milk cows. The heifers are freshening, so don't know exactly how many they milk. They have a lot of cows to feed too. They grind hay for the animals in the barn, and also the straw they use in there - plus they grind their own feed. Those screenings sure cost a lot nowadays. They are also mechanics so have no dull moments. They have a Bobcat in the garage right now to repair, and also a car. David hauls cattle to Fargo to the ring whenever he gets a load - was there last week, and three times the week before. We really have such a busy pace -but guess that's the price you pay for having such a big family, and we love it.

This past week was one of those weeks. Ryan was here all day yesterday. Ron and Karen left at seven for Fargo, got home last night after ten, were here until eleven-thirty. Jerry was making his first freezer of ice cream and they enjoyed it with us. Ryan was just thirteen on December 12, and you wouldn't believe his size . He's taller than his father and wears a size 12-E shoe. He's not fat, just tall. He will be lots bigger. He's our youngest grandson; there are only two girls younger, A.M.'s Angela and Jim's Tracey, both ten. But we sure have lots of great-grandchildren. Dot has 19 grandchildren and only seven are girls, the rest boys, the oldest to turn twelve in January. Must be lots of action when they come over to her house, which they do often as they live close by. They go to her house on Christmas Eve. The rest of our kids come over, but the married grandkids (besides hers) go to their in-laws....

Here's another Christmas letter, four years later:

Hi,
    You know, Rose, I still feel like you are still Rosie-Re. Like when you were a tot. But I guess we have all grown up a lot since then. I got Bill to write a few lines to his bachelor brothers in Iowa last night. He claimed he couldn't write any more, but his letter was readable if not very long, but it will give Walter and Emil much pleasure.

    Son Billy and his wife Nikki and BJ left for Florida this morning; anyway they were going if the weather didn't look stormy. BJ stands for Billie Joanne. She is thirteen. Nikki's dad has some sickness and is in and out of the hospital. So they thought they'd go see him once more.

They made our Christmas program at church last fall before it got so cold. Our churches don't have enough kids so they all helped. They acted out the whole Christmas story, were dressed for the parts and everything. They made slides and Nikki showed them on the screen, while the three last girls were confirmed last Sunday read the story. Our three ten year-olds each read a part of it from the pulpit. It sure was nice - we had Corey, four, Tiffany and Kris, age five, besides those three girls. They sang three Christmas songs real nice. Their teachers sure are talented. Kids are such a blessing but some of these teen grandchildren sure need lots of prayer. Hopefully they will turn out OK.

When you mention Waterloo, Iowa, that is a place Bill knew real well when he lived in Iowa. Ronnie works for a machine company; they haul stuff all over Iowa and Minnesota. He is sometimes gone for two days at a time. They live next door to us. Billy and Jim work in a shop in Cooper. Billy and Chuck own their old home farm, but rent most of the farm out. Chuck sells AAL insurance.

Much love,
Alice

I must pause here and tell you a little about Hazel, who I think represents the best of North Dakota womanhood. It was Hazel's place to which I was hired one summer as a harvest helpmate; it was Hazel who taught me so much about being strong both emotionally and physically. She was of Norwegian descent, and I respected her completely for what she was, and still is. She was the one who made things happen - whether on the farm, in the house, at the church, within or without the family - and it was always in an orderly, organized fashion. Some people did not particularly like her administrative ways, but everyone respected her because she got things done. And - to my recollection - I never heard her say anything negative about anyone. She had the confidence and strength to just get things done.

These were hard times for my parents; they weren't happy with the situation, and the Depression had by then bitten into the land with the fiercest grip in history. Dad, who'd so hoped he could farm those few acres with some success, learned quickly the land was poor, and clotted with rocks. The fields would have to be cleared, a mammoth effort in good times, impossible in bad. To my recollection, I think they tried - but the rocks just broke the machinery and they gave it up. And then there was the famous drought of those years, and the legendary dust bowl winds. But we did have the Leininger farms all around us and the labor they required really helped. Dad worked with Uncle John and Uncle Michael plowing, planting, threshing, and he taught school for a time too, so we never lacked for anything, even in those mean years.

What money we had came from Dad's farm labors, which I think he enjoyed, and his teaching in our little school, which he probably also enjoyed. And we all benefitted (even Mother, I'm sure) from being so close to Dad's large and warm extended family. We had so few standards to judge by back then. Only a few people had a radio and we rarely saw a magazine or an advertisement, so we didn't know what we were supposed to be wanting, or what we were supposed to want to look like. For all its "poverty", ours was a simple and wholesome life.

Perhaps I should pause here and explain a little about how our Lutheran religion affected our lives. Even though my father was an ordained preacher, religion was never obsessive in our home. We went to church, we had devotions every night after supper, we prayed at meals and at night as a family. That probably seems like a lot to many people, but it was all we knew so we never complained. We went to vacation bible school in the summer, we went to Walther League camp when we were a little older, and we went to confirmation classes when we were about fourteen or so, so we could be "confirmed" as members. These classes took about two years to get through, and were held on Saturday mornings. We did a lot of memorization of certain hymns, biblical verses and of course the entire catechism which was called "The Six Chief Parts." When we'd accomplished all that, and recited it back without mistakes, then we were confirmed as worthy members of the church.

But even though we practiced our religion to a devout degree, and remember the sermons, the scriptures, the devotions, the prayers when I think about our pastoral home. What I recall best, and with great fondness, is a little poem Dad used to say, regardless of the time or season - it seemed he just liked to say it, as though the sounds of the words soothed him. I have struggled and struggled as I've been writing this book, to remember all the words.

One of my fondest memories of my dad is of the sound of his voice, saying this little poem, perhaps on some golden afternoon when we were alone, maybe milking the cow, or just walking; it seems to me now to be so typical of him at his "best" self, the dear man I loved. I remember one occasion particularly well; it was when he and Mother were staying with me in their later years. One day he stood at my kitchen window and repeated it again, but with such sadness and feeling of loss, which I did not connect with his life until I began this book.

"The leaves are fading and falling,
The winds are rough and wild,
The birds have ceased their calling,
But let me tell you, my child,
When these bright days are over,
And the forests lose their leaves,
We wept for one so lovely,
Who had a life so brief..."

Chapter Two

"Oh Give Me a Home, Where the Buffalo Roam...."

Home...the dearest, and most magical word, I think; dearest because it conjures up such precious images of love and warmth and place, and magical because it means a myriad of different memories in each mind that has ever been. And even though we may live in dozens of places in our lifetimes, there is only one place, one image, which is home. I lived in the country in a small town in my childhood, but they are all the same place they are all one welcoming memory every time I say the word.

I was just a little girl about two years old when we moved to Binford in 1933, so I don't remember a lot about that place specifically, except that Dad farmed land he inherited from his father and he didn't preach in those years. I was about seven when we left there to settle in Deep (actually just a train depot and some grain elevators) some 200 miles west, in 1938; it was here that I lived out my most active childhood years. We moved to Kensal in 1945, and it was the first really bona fide <u>town</u> I lived in; it was back near the eastern border of the state. I was about fourteen then, and just beginning to bound my way through those trying adolescent years of zinging harmonies, pesky pimples and the strange newness <u>boys</u> had suddenly taken on. But despite the moves there is really only one image of "home" in my mind, because each of the three houses were similar in character, and now they have all melded together in my mind. "Home" was always sweet to me - it is 'til this day, though you'll wonder why when I tell you how we lived in "Home Sweet Home" North Dakota style!

Every house we lived in was the same: white, frame, two story - a box of a house. This is what most people lived in up there, probably because no other building materials were available, and additions could easily be made to accommodate growing families. Most families had a separate living room and dining room with maybe a wooden folding door between them, or some book shelves, or some French doors. Most furniture was considered "functional" but the parlor furniture was usually fairly nice, if possible. I remember in our house we had little plaques around the house with English and German sayings on them. Considered sacred, the family only used these rooms on special occasions when "company" came. For most families, life revolved around the kitchen because food was the center of our lives, the centerpiece of nearly every social occasion. Like most families, we ate in the kitchen (in winter it was the warmest place in the house), or on a large enclosed porch in warmer months. In those days too, you used to have Sears Roebuck mail order houses. The largest and most famous catalogue mail order retail company offered, through their catalogues, the first "pre-fab" houses. There were a number of sizes and plans; the simplest "Prairie Home" could be had for about $595.00 - the most elaborate, with two stories and stained glass windows and built in china cabinets, for about

$5,000. So if you were handy, you could build yourself a nice house by following the instructions! (Most farm families also had regular visits from traveling salesmen, like the Fuller Brush man, the Watkins man, and the Raleigh man, who sold things like spices, vanilla, brushes, brooms, and other household cleaning products.)

And speaking of heat - there was never enough of it! Maybe I remember that because I've always been cold blooded, but I know it was true up there where winter lasted from October to May. And remember furnaces were not what they are now. I remember in our house in Deep, the main heater was in the middle of the living room, which was also Dad's study. We'd stand around that in the mornings while we got dressed - it was definitely the warmest place in the house. Otherwise, the furnace in the cellar would provide heat through vents in the first floor. There were no ducts further up except for those directly above the first floor's vents. What we got upstairs was through this one duct in each room; there were none in the halls.

Mother would heat up old flat irons or bricks on the wood burning kitchen stove, which we wrapped in towels and put in our beds to warm the covers. We'd leave them under there all night and they'd keep us pretty warm - except I was never warm enough! When it was really, really cold, Mother and Dad brought the beds downstairs and set them up in their room on the first floor, or in the parlor/study. I must add too that hot water came not from a tap, but a big pot or kettle on the wood burning kitchen stove. (One of our stoves had big metal reservoir on the side which, if kept filled, would always provide a fair supply of warm water. But Mom always made us rinse the dishes with boiling tea kettle water; for her, this was the only proper way to rinse dishes.) Baths meant several kettlesful of hot water poured into a big metal tub in which we each had our turn; one tub had to do for all three or four of us kids. Lucky was he or she who got to bathe first! Tudy, being the youngest, usually had that privilege.

We four girls were assigned one bedroom upstairs, two to a double bed. Poor Bob, being the only son and heir, had to sleep alone in his own private room - a privilege we girls protested mightily but fruitlessly; there was simply no other way to do it, as we never had more than three bedrooms. Each girl had one drawer in the two chests of drawers, and we shared the closet in which we had our designated space for dresses and coats. For some unknown reason Mother relegated Lois and me to the same double bed, an arrangement we heartily disliked because I was always cold and Lois wasn't. We had to share the warm iron, if you can imagine, so we were always arguing about who got to rub toes on the iron, and who was touching whom. Hardly a night passed without Lois grumbling "Quit <u>touching</u> me! Stay on <u>your</u> side of the bed!", and I insisting, "I'm not touching you!" or "Quit hogging all the covers!"

None of us liked this enforced coziness, but when I look back on those years now I realize we were blessed to share those sisterly bedtimes. Sure we committed our share of bedtime high jinx and romping antics; but we also talked amongst ourselves, "girltalk," you know, the special kind that only sisters have. I really missed my big sisters Dorothy and Lois when they went away for their last years of high school. One thing has never left me though, and that's my inability to never feel warm enough! Fortunately for me, both my first husband Walter and Don, my second (I was widowed very young), have been very generous in letting me sleep as close to them as I want at night. Don even makes sure the electric blanket is turned up high enough for me!

If this sounds a bit rough, keep reading; it gets rougher. Of course we had no indoor toilets; few did out in the country. Everyone had an outside facility - an "outhouse" - and ours was usually a two holer, though some had four holes. It was never a joy to go in there; not only was the business itself unpleasant, but there always lurked the possibility of a snake, or any other kind of creature a child could imagine.

And toilet paper? Though it was something of a small luxury in those Depression days, Mother always made sure we had some. But when we went visiting, we might find anything in the visited outhouse. Usually it was the Montgomery Ward or the Sears Roebuck catalogues, and the pages of these worked pretty well if you crumpled them up good. But if the yellowed pages were gone, we were goners too! And there certainly wasn't a sink and running water anywhere near. The next best thing was the water trough for the stock, usually around pretty close. Mom would often carry a small roll of paper in her purse, but she wasn't always around when we needed it. In bitter weather though, it was hard going just to get out there through the snow. So Dad rigged up a seat in the basement, under which he put a large can. We'd go there until it was full (oh, the stench!), and then Dad took it out to the outhouse.

While we may not have enjoyed going there, we kids did get a thrill out of watching someone <u>else</u> go, for a l-o-n-g time. It was just a matter of turning a wooden knob, ever so quietly, and waiting until imprisonment was discovered. This happened rather frequently at our house when we had company or visiting relatives; it even happened to one of the visiting preachers, most embarrassing for my folks, not to mention the victim. But the identity of the pranksters remains a secret to this day - and, I suspect, will remain so for some decades to come!

While it's hard to imagine today, we had no electricity until I was 14, when we moved to Kensal in 1945. In all our first homes we used gas lamps which were hung from the ceiling, or kerosene lamps which we carried from room to room. It was quite a trick to get the gas lamps started; Dad allowed no one but himself to tackle it, as it was considered a dangerous task. He had to pump the air into the lamp, then light the little mantles which flared up into instant brightness. We also used kerosene lanterns, which we carried outside for chore time, like when we fed the chickens or milked the cow. I remember washing the black soot from the chimneys on Saturday, when we all did chores. We had to be especially careful because the glass was fragile and easy to break. You can imagine how thrilling it was for us when we finally got electricity, to just flip a little switch and find ourselves immediately bathed in light!

We did have a telephone though, even if it was a bit primitive. It was just like the old ones you often see in old movies: a wooden cabinet with a speaking tube and that old funnel shaped bell thing we listened through. If you wanted to call someone, you'd ring up the local operator and tell her the number you wanted to call, and she'd connect you. If you wanted to pass important information to a number of people, the operator would ring up all the people with one long ring, and everyone picked up their phone. There was a code of rings so the party in question would know the call was for them. (Two shorts and a long, for example.) But you could pick up the phone at any time and listen in to anyone who was talking without their knowing it - perfect grapevine, though in those days we called it rubbering. We were warned to refrain from such!

Refrigeration was also just a concept until we moved to Kensal. Most of the time we got our water from a cistern, which Dorothy reminds me not infrequently had mice in it, so we didn't use it for drinking, just washing, etc. (She also reminds me that we often had lizards in the cellar and in Kensal there were snakes hanging from the ceiling!!) For drinking water we had to go to the well, always away from the house; we brought it back to the house in buckets. To this day Cousin Alice keeps her bucket in the same place with the same "community" dipper nearby, with narry a thought for germs!

For most families out where we lived, the refrigerator was the great outdoors. Since the climate was cold or at least cool so much of the year, we used the back porch to keep things cold. To freeze a batch of mousse, Dad would set it in a snow bank for us to enjoy when it had hardened up. So delicious! You know, I got so used to putting things "out on the back porch" that years later, when I was first married and had a small refrigerator, I kept a cooked roast in a cupboard "out on the porch", for seven days! I was so sure it wouldn't need the 'fridge; Mother had kept meat that way, hadn't she ? Can you imagine how it smelled?

32

Some of the folks we knew kept their milk and butter chilled in their cisterns. Farmers used a gas engine to pump water from their well during the summer. Others would haul in big ice blocks from town which they'd store in the modern refrigerator's predecessor, the ice box. We always used what they called a "locker". We'd rent a freezer locker at the meat market in town, and there we'd keep whatever meats we fell heir to, either by purchase or gift. It cost us about $20 a month, which was a large sum in those day. Dad was always the one to go to town and get what we needed out of the locker.

Seems like I talk about food a lot, but it really was the "Staff of Life" for farming people who grew it and sold it - as well as ate it. Food marked the high points of our daily lives through the weeks, months and years. Any meal was an occasion: big noon-time dinners for farm folk marked half a day's labor done; a summer barbecue with cake and home-made ice cream might celebrate the country's birthday or a cousin's; and holiday feasts always signaled thanks for hearth and family and God's blessings. And since neighbors often lived miles apart, any visit at all between us was cause for welcome in the form of warm pie and coffee, and every good housewife always had a pie or cake or caramel rolls on hand for "company", unless we were all snowed in by a blizzard. (But it took a blizzard to halt production!)

Mom did most of the cooking and baking, no small task for a family of seven. She'd make up a batch of four loaves of bread at a time - bread you would kill for, it was so delicious. She'd pull it out of the oven when the crust was just slightly hard, crunchy enough on the outside, and soft white clouds of sheer heaven inside. It was hard to cut the first day; you had to saw it just right so the white wouldn't get squashed. We'd usually do it all wrong in our haste to taste the first morsel, and then, toward the end of the loaf the last few slices would get crooked. It took Mom or Dad to carefully slice off pieces from the heel. We'd all fight for the first slice still warm soaked in fresh butter...<u>nothing</u> tasted better, not even caramel rolls.

By the end of four loaves (not very long), we weren't fighting for the crust anymore, so Mother and Dad ate what we didn't want. To this day, I associate the hard crust with my parents - and other parents. I vividly remember watching a visiting pastor eating all the left overs on his children's plates! "Waste not, Want not" was a motto taken very seriously, even though food was plentiful for social occasions. At our house, if the meal was, say chili, there'd be a big pot of it for seven people, and we each got one serving; that was <u>all</u>. If you were very lucky, and there was a little bit left, you might get a tiny portion more.

33

Dad helped a lot in the kitchen, all his life, even when he was very old. The youngest child of eight, he was a "liberated" husband long before it became fashionable in the 1980s. He did certain things because he was good at them - like "Johnny Cake", which was cornbread, and he also made the pancakes. So we grew up watching our father work in the kitchen - unusual for men of his time, but very normal, and expected for us. I think back now on all the things we ate and wonder how we five kids, anyway, managed to stay so thin - and we were regular bean poles, like our parents.

Mother and other women in the area used to bake up the most wonderful caramel rolls - and I have yet to taste their equal. Of course there was plenty of butter and cream available and most folks used plenty of it. Lard was easy to get and was used primarily for frying meat, since it didn't burn. Some also made soap from it.

Our days always started with a big breakfast - usually hot cooked cereal, toast and milk, sometimes juice. Mother fixed this while we were jumping into our clothes around the best source of heat in our house at the time, usually a stove in Daddy's study. It seems to me now that we ate an enormous amount at breakfast, but we needed it for the long walk to school, which started at nine. When weather was nice, we walked across the field and down the rail road tracks, but when it snowed, we had one other option - Dad's car. Dad would put hot coals under the engine at night to keep it warm so it would start the next day; but sometimes it was just too cold, and we walked a half mile over the frozen fields, and then another mile down the rail road tracks to our one room school. (We might have twenty kids on a good day.) Actually, the walk wasn't so bad - one of my most cherished memories is of crunching over those sun-blasted snow-packed fields on those frigid mornings. It was so beautiful! We never felt any hardship because we had to walk to school; it was just something we did.

I'll have more to say about our school days later, but I must tell you now about - of course - our lunches. (I told you food was important to us!) In my first school years, we all brought our lunch (usually sandwiches) in buckets, but later we had hot lunches provided through some federal act which allowed us to use government surplus goods like butter, cheese and other staples. At one time we had a cook come to the school. Once she used a pressure cooker to cook some bean soup for us - but it exploded and sprayed beans all over the place! We loved it, but the poor cook was humiliated as well as burned; and then we felt bad, of course. But it was an unforgettable lunch.

After school we'd walk home via the same route, dawdling maybe along the tracks or along the ditches looking for trouble. By the time we got home we were pretty tired and hungry. And what a joy it was to walk along knowing Mother would <u>always</u> be there, ready with a snack for us. When it was in season, we had fruit, but most of the time we had our favorite snack of ketchup bread. Lest you faint dead away of revulsion, I must remind you that flour and tomato products were things farm folks always had in good supply; everybody made their own bread, and canned up their homegrown tomatoes in sauces, soups, juices, ketchup and the like. And anyway, when you're a kid you're entitled to like strange combinations, right? Well, we kids <u>loved</u> ketchup sandwiches.

After some chores, we'd help Mother with supper. She usually did most of the major jobs, like mashing the potatoes, mixing the meat loaf. We'd help with smaller tasks like chopping onions, peeling potatoes, setting the table. Mother taught each of us to learn to do one dish as our best. I was best at mixing tapioca pudding, I remember, and Lois did chocolate pudding. Most of our suppers had some kind of meat - maybe pork chops or chicken, and potatoes in some form or another. In season we had fresh garden vegetables; in winter we had green beans, peas, maybe corn my folks had canned themselves the previous summer, or carrots we'd stored in sand in the cellar. After supper we all helped wash dishes, a chore we all despised - but more on that later. When dinner was cleared we'd do our homework around the table, or practice the piano.

We all had beginning lessons on the piano, but of the girls only Dorothy and Tudy took to it. Bob became an excellent pianist, though, took lessons all through his growing up years from Dad and eventually earned a Master's degree in musicology. He later learned to play the organ as well, but when I think about Bob and piano, I always hum the piece I loved to hear him play best, "Malaguenya" - which was a monster to play, demanding chords ten keys apart!! (I could barely reach an octave!)

Our clothes were pretty basic: one pair of pants (for the girls) with a sweater, a few dresses, everyday shoes, sunday shoes - and that was about it. Playclothes were just old school outfits that had lost their "propriety" for public use. When we were little, Mother made simple dresses and aprons out of flour sacks, and of course we wore each other's hand-me-downs. Bob usually got new things when he outgrew the old - how we envied him that! He never had to watch something come down through two or three sisters before he got it. Even his hand-me-downs from cousins were "newer" than ours. Whatever we outgrew we took over to the kin in Binford where even hand-me-downs were welcome in those big families.

And oh, all the <u>stuff</u> we girls had to wear in those days! Start with long underwear (down to wrists and ankles), then petticoats, then skirt and sweater or dress. Then long brown stockings, held up by a garter belt, and "sensible" brown shoes, always bought at least a size too large so we'd get good use out of them. Outer gear was a heavy coat or the snow suit as I've described, with ugly rubber boots that snapped up the front.

The only really good clothes we had were the special outfits our Indianapolis grandmother sent to us from the Big City; "clothes for good" as she always called them. I was only six when she died, so I never really knew her, but the nice clothes kept coming. After her death Grandfather Behrmann acquired what my parents referred to as "a friend of the female gender", who for years continued to send us nice clothes for special occasions. She also sent the most exquisitely decorated candies for Christmas and Easter. We kids just <u>knew</u> she was rich - she had to be to buy these incredible morsels of heaven for us; and our friends teased us about being rich. You can imagine how we looked forward to her big boxes full of lovely clothes and candied treasures. I don't even recall her name, but the packages continued until Grandfather's death.

Since our "wardrobes" were limited, we had to wash clothes often. As far back as I remember, we had what we called a washer. It was a cumbersome machine with the washer itself, a wringer that looked like two rolling pins, and two side tubs for rinsing. (Later Dad made a stand for the rinsing tubs so that Mother wouldn't have to bend over so much.) We soaked the clothes overnight, and the next day we'd agitate them in the washer's soapy water, then fold them up just wide enough to feed them through the wringer (which could easily wring your hands if you weren't careful, and did once in a while.) We rinsed them twice, and used bluing in those days to make white things brighter - very important for a preacher's collars! We kept the washer out on the back porch, but some of our relatives moved theirs out under a shade tree for the summer, close to a clothes line. Dad would bring in a boiler full of snow, which we heated on the stove to near boiling, to which we added water from the hot tea kettle to keep the water hot through numerous loads of wash. We washed once a week, usually on Monday, and it was a day long affair which demanded help from all of us.

As I remember, the white things were washed first, then the colored things, and lastly the heavy work clothes. We used lye soap - no commercially made powder then - and until we got our washing machine, the clothes had to be scrubbed on a corrugated metal board. When we were little, sometimes we'd "help" by scrubbing the handkerchiefs. Then the wet things were rung out, by a ringer if you were lucky to have one, by hand if you weren't. Can you imagine wringing out heavy overalls and blankets by hand?!

Another bit about a special washboard - the one I took with me through my DMLC years, my LPN training years and my three years of nursing school - and all through my adult years, wherever I've lived. What would I have done without it in the years of nursing and all those spotless white uniforms? I can well remember my poor mother, bending over the wash tub scrubbing the clothes for five, six, eventually seven people - all on a scrub board. And every white piece we wore was spotless, no gray. Whereas my laundry greys with repeated washing in an electric automatic washer and dryer - I don't have <u>time</u> for that kind of attention, but then Mother didn't either! I found my little wash board just the other day in a box in my basement. Dusty and more than a little grimy, I noticed there was something written on the wood near the top where the soap sits. I cleaned it up and read the "Directions: Do not rub hard. The board will do the work." It even has a name - "The Zing King"; don't you love it? Sounds like a fast food joint, or maybe a badminton set. But there was more - some pale handwriting near the top - "Leininger". What else?

Anyway, back to wash day. Now we get to the drying! When the weather was nice, we'd hang everything outside. But in North Dakota where winters are long and the temperatures usually below freezing for months at a time, we had to devise other methods. Colored clothes were hung on lines in the basement, or in some homes, in the parlor or the bedrooms. The white clothes were hung on racks or clothes lines outside so they would freeze. I don't know why - perhaps to keep them looking white. When we brought these in from outside, the house seemed to get colder, since they now had to be hung inside to dry enough to iron. So you can imagine just how accomplished we felt when wash day was done! How fresh the sheets smelled as we made the beds that evening!

I remember Dad being home a lot. He'd do a lot of visiting during the days, when he could, but mostly he was around. Mother was almost always there. Frequently she'd host the Ladies' Aid meetings at our house, or she might go to a quilting bee or something like that but she was <u>always</u> home when we got home from school. I know Dad was a real help to her because he'd do a lot of work around the house. In certain ways, we dealt more with our father than our mother on a daily basis, because she was so busy with the housework. She couldn't bother herself with our squabbles, our various crimes and misdemeanors, so Dad took on the job of disciplinarian, and believe me, his word was Law. We <u>never</u> said bad words. If we said "darn" or "gosh" within his hearing, he'd only say 'Whaaaaat?!" and we'd pipe down right now. Anything even remotely similar to

37

God's name might warrant a punishment. And if Dad wasn't around, and my mother heard it, she'd say, "Just wait until your father gets home!" We knew we were in for it.

But we could always talk to him about anything we needed - like homework, even religion - but likewise we respected his private time. We knew he needed to study. I think we all found certain times in the day when we knew we could go to him. My special time was when he went to the barn to milk the cow. I'd sit there on a little stool and we'd talk to the rhythmic spurts of warm milk hitting the side of the pail. I loved those times with him.

Mother was a very hard worker, and I have always loved her for the good qualities she had. But it took many years for me to really understand how deep her sad loneliness was, and to empathize with the degree of her endurance through what for her were some very difficult and unhappy times. She never was able to feel the rewards of self confidence and financial security. She always submitted to Dad's direction, which in a way made her the perfect wife for a clergyman who was trained in the ways women, particularly his, should behave in the living of a "righteous" life. They passed this submissiveness on to us three older girls, who also married pastors. Eventually, I <u>think</u> I've managed to mold myself after Hazel; certainly I feel better about myself and my life than poor Mother ever did. My heart aches to this day for her unhappiness.

We took it for granted that we'd go to church on Sunday...there was Sunday School first, and then worship service. Sometimes the service would be in German; I can remember sitting there in the pew, trying to figure out the foreign words in the little black hymnal. Sometimes Dad had a "preaching station", which meant he had to fill in for another preacher in some nearby town or hamlet. So he'd drive miles to another church for the afternoon; Sundays were often very long for him. Later there would be meetings for the Walther Leagues for the youth, choir practice, Sunday School meetings, and other church related meetings which required his supervision. He really was a very busy man, as I suppose any man of God must of necessity be.

Dad also had to go to regional meetings every so often. They called them pastoral conferences, and they were all day affairs in some distant town or in a country home. Often wives were supposed to go too, and when we were little they took us with them for those long tedious meetings. But despite the fact that Dad was a minister, I never felt like religion ruled our lives. We read from our family bible or a devotion book every evening after supper, we had daily prayer over meals, and certain well used prayers we said absolutely every night. But they were a part of our lives - and the lives of everyone we knew. We never knew any different, so never thought there were other ways to live.

Of course this was through the later years of the Depression, which began in 1929 and dragged on through the next decade until World War II began in 1939, and then the United States' entry into it late in 1941. Times were terrible, especially in the early thirties, when drought and poor markets nearly destroyed many farmers. Yet I don't remember a single farm family losing their farm; the banks would let them pay their loans back a little at a time. I do remember getting a lot of bartered goods - food instead of cash. And homeless, wandering men we called "bums" would sometimes come to the back door and ask for food and a place to sleep in the barn. To this day I remember Mother feeding them on steaming plates at the back cellar door. Sometimes they offered to do some chore for their meals, and I think Dad had them do something around the place.

Nobody had money then, and since members didn't, we didn't. There was no guaranteed salary during the Depression in the Lutheran ministry, a fact my mother is quick to point out to any of her grandchildren who might think about becoming a preacher. I know she was especially hard pressed in those years to keep the family going on so little. In the early years I remember there being big cloth sacks of flour, which we stored in our attic in Binford. Mother would say, "Well, we won't starve, we've got flour in the attic." So we had lots of wonderful bread from the flour and play clothes from the sacks - and never wanted for anything. Occasionally a member would slip Dad a $10 bill, for which he was very grateful. He'd tell us of this member's kindness, and we were sure they must be rich; you had to be rich to give away so <u>much</u> money! Odd now, isn't it? that over fifty years later I sit in my well stocked and appointed suburban kitchen and look back on those times with such longing. Those truly were good old days, but perhaps only for us children whose only task was to grow up healthy and happy, which we did, for the most part.

Going to town on Saturday was probably <u>the</u> highlight of the week for us; it was the day we'd bring in our eggs and butter to sell, and then we'd buy some staple we needed. We almost always had a cow on the place, so whatever butter and eggs we didn't use, we'd sell in town. I remember one time we got nearly to town only to discover my folks had left the eggs at home! So they drove all the way back, eight miles, to get them.

When we lived in the country near Deep, "town" was Newburg, some eight miles away, where we bought most of our groceries, and we kids spent our allowance which was smaller. (As we got older, it was fifty cents a week.) We loved going to town because we knew we'd get some kind of treat, preferably a nickel ice cream cone, or an ice cream bar. Sometimes we'd get a five cent cupcake. Later on we adored twenty cent (so much money!) malted milks. When times were really bad and loose change was scarce, Mother would buy one candy bar and split it in five pieces. One stick of gum got divided into four pieces, each of which just disintegrated after a few chews, or else got swallowed without us even noticing. I know I lost my little wad often enough in the small corners of my mouth my tongue never found. If more sticks were available, Mother would divide it in thirds; a half-stick allotment was very extravagant. And do you know? Well into my adult years a full piece of gum still felt wasteful, in fact, cumbersome; all that sticky wad rolling around in my mouth. For years I never allowed myself a full stick; chewing it looked unladylike, and anyway, I always felt guilty for taking so much!

Saturday night Mother would get out the curling iron. Despite our profoundly straight fair hair, which was usually cut in a dutch boy style, she tried weekly to have us look a little more angelic on the Sabbath. It must have taken her hours to do all of us girls; in those days you held the rod (remember, no electricity) in the heat of a lamp flame until it was hot enough, and then you'd roll up the hair, one curl at a time. Mom was very patient and tried to be careful, but we usually came away with burned ears and necks, the price of beauty on the prairies. When we got older we went to town for a permanent once a year, for $2 a piece. In the early days of permanents, the hair was wound up on special rollers which then were attached to electricity for thirty minutes! Later came chemical perms, but no perm is ever a pleasant experience.

I must add here that it was during our time in Deep that I first knew my present husband, Don Brauer. Don was the youngest of five sons of a Lutheran preacher in Minot, North Dakota, to us a "big city" about fifty miles from Deep on a gravel road. Of course my parents knew the Brauers well so there was a lot of socializing between the families; between their five boys and our four girls (and Bob) you can be sure we kept things fairly volatile when we got together. I first developed a relationship with Don when we were both about five years old. What struck me about him was that he was perfectly willing to play paper dolls if I wanted to, as well as boy games. It just seemed the thing to do when you were five...and anyway was a little more acclimated than most boys to girl things, I supposed as I was more acclimated than most girls to boy things.

So our childhoods were laced together with friendly ties of companionship and equality - and when we met again years later, we could build on what we'd begun, and it felt right. By fifth grade though, the Brauers moved to Monango, a little town south of Jamestown, where he lived through high school and was valedictorian of his class. Later he left to go to Concordia College, River Forest, Illinois, a suburb of Chicago.

Another dear friend I knew in those Deep years was Lori Hall Duesenberg, whose family owned and worked a large farm not far from Newburg. They attended the Lutheran church in Deep River, and through church oriented activities we came to know each other, even though Lori was seven years younger than I. Our friendship really blossomed when, years later, Dad was hospitalized where she was working at Lutheran Hospital in St. Louis where we both now live. Lori's Mother still lives on the family farm, in the same house (now modernized), and they go to the same little white frame "American Gothic" Lutheran church in Deep River. One of Lori's brothers built another house on the property, and continues to farm the family acreage.

As we grew in size and ability, Mother taught us how to wash, dry and put away the dishes her way. I think I could safely say that from the time we were big enough to stand on a chair pulled up to the sink to the very day we left home for adulthood, we were doing dishes - and hating every moment of it. We hated this chore almost more than any other, perhaps because it was endless - another meal, another batch of dirty plates, glasses, silverware, pots and pans. It was at these times of the day that our real hard core hand to hand fighting occurred, or hand to mouth I should say, because we threw and spat water at each other with a vengeance. Poor Mother must have hated it as much as we did because of all the fighting - but there was nothing she could do to stop it, no matter what the threat. Of course it was always done more subtlety when Dad was "in the other room" studying. Threats to "tell your father" usually quelled us somewhat until we finished the dreaded chore. It didn't matter whose turn it was to do what (washing, rinsing, drying, stacking), it was always an unpleasant task for all five of us (Bob did them too), it rarely ended happily. Of course I can look back on those times with plenty of smiles now, and if I try very hard, I can almost miss them!

And then there were Saturdays, and what we had to do before we got to go to town. To Mother, Saturday cleaning was an absolute right up there with the Ten Commandments, and it could no more be skipped than curls and church on Sunday. Unfortunately for us, Mother's big city upbringing demanded a fastidiously kept house. Fortunately for Mother, the Lord had provided her with five able if unwilling helpers in her never ending quest for a clean and "godly" house. We not only had to clean everything (dust, scrub, run the Bissell carpet sweeper, straighten, wash, etc.), we had to clean it thoroughly (re-dust, re-scrub, re-wash, etc.) until she approved. We all had our assigned tasks, and as I recall we rotated the worst chore, like scrubbing the kitchen floor, and washing down all the kitchen cabinets. Well, you can imagine that the feathers flew between four girls and one boy, literally as well as figuratively. We staged terrific pillow fights, and fired tremendous salvos of shoes up and down the stairs. We were merciless and our ammunition of anger endless; in fact it deepened with each passing year. But Mother held firm: no playing, no reading, no trip to town unless the whole house sparkled; even the plate rail along the kitchen wall had to be dusted!

And of course, everywhere we lived we put in a big garden; all country folk did. We put in potatoes, carrots, beans, peas, corn, beets, cucumbers, tomatoes, squash, onions - and always a row of hollyhocks, to beautify, and marigolds, whose unpleasant scent kept raiding varmints away. A glorious flower patch was usually just part of any self respecting country gardener; so you had not only luscious fruits and vegetables, but also lovely bouquets inside on the dinner table. Dad loved flowers and so the flower garden was his special domain. He was very creative too, and would fashion interesting designs like stars or circles out of zinnias, marigolds, hollyhocks, snapdragons, cosmos, petunias...and there were usually morning glories too, climbing up something.

The glorious spring and summer months meant extra chores, of course; not all things green and growing were welcome. One of our most dreaded chores in summer was weeding the garden, always arduous work because the soil was often dry and the weed roots stubborn. Watering the garden wasn't much fun either, because we had to haul the water by the bucketful in our little red wagon, and this meant many trips every day when the weather was dry.

When the season was good to us, our garden yielded bountiful amounts of produce, and that meant even more work for us kids when we were older. I think my folks learned early on that an eight year old does not have the coordination to pull pea pods gently from the vine. Since we usually uprooted the whole thing, Mother and Dad did the picking, but set us to the task of shucking corn, shelling the peas, snapping the green beans, washing the beets, the tomatoes...either getting them ready to eat or to can for winter's use.

Canning was definitely a family affair, and when certain things were ready - say we'd gathered a big bushel of tomatoes - then we'd set up our canning routine, and take our stations at certain parts of the process. Somebody would wash the tomatoes, dip them in a kettle of boiling water, skin them, then pack the newly washed mason jars (someone else's job) with quartered tomatoes and seal them with caps and rings. Then we'd settle six or eight quart jars of them into a large canner for an hour at least until they were safely sealed and preserved. The process was pretty similar for most of the other things too, unless we were making juice or ketchup or jams and jellies. When they were in season, we bought lots of peaches, pears and sometimes apricots to can, so we'd have fruit and steaming cobblers and pies all winter.

42

Canning days were always fussy days for everyone. It would be a day long affair, and it was hot; awful, really, in the summer heat. We'd bicker about who got what job, and whatever job we had was the worst one, so we'd complain about it. "But I did this last time, it's your turn to wash jars!" We'd squabble about who wasn't being "nice", and who we were going to "tell" on, and we teased back and forth until water flew - and the folks descended.

But the best memories I have of those summertimes have to do with the flowers. Just the barest whiff of lilac sends me flying back over miles and years to those heavy, stately plumes of lilac bushes that burst forth every spring in every place we lived. I have always <u>loved</u> lilacs...and peonies, which popped those little marble-sized fists into showy, petaled orbs of pink and red and white just a few weeks later. Lilacs and peonies were standard accouterments to country living. So much so that when a couple married, friends might give the newlyweds some good clumps of each to decorate the church. I remember when Dorothy got married we were living in Kensal, peonies were one of her wedding gifts, given by a couple with generous hearts. We had the reception on our lawn and the peonies had bloomed in perfect time for the occasion...I will always think of that day as one of the happiest I've known, because the family was happy, Dorothy was so beautiful and her Wally so handsome; the reception was beautiful and fragrant with peonies - and love. Oh yes, I remember that day - because I was nineteen, my braces had come off, I knew I was looking pretty - and it was that day that I fell in "love" with my first real guy. His name was Bill and he was one of the groomsmen, a good friend of Dorothy's husband Wally. He was a gorgeous hunk...but that's a tale to save for later. Now it's time to check the barn!

Chapter Three

*"Oh Beautiful for Spacious Skies
For Amber Waves of Grain..."*

Whenever I think of North Dakota, I think of summer, because for me, it was our most beautiful time of year, and most precious since the warm months were so few. And even though I never lived on a real working farm (just close to my Uncle John's in Binford), I've always thought of myself as a country girl, because I was in love with it - the torrid sun, the merciless wind heavy with pungent green smells, the fields heaving with waves of wheat. I could never get enough of summer...I look back on that skinny, towheaded waif that was I and realize now how intense she was, how possessed by summer's magic. Fevered, she drank daily at summer's sweet rim, drank it dry, in fact, of its potent nectar; and yet her thirst begged for more, as unslaked as those rocky pastures.

She'd get up early on summer mornings, to find some chore to do, or game to play, or mischief to get into - anything to be outside and taking in all the romance of Sssssummer! For there was no other word for it; she was in love. Oh, she loved how the sunlight stood straight up at noon, and all the flowers saluted in their brightest colors; she loved how our few trees drowsed by mid-afternoon, tossing, nodding over checker games on the back porch. But the time she loved the best was just before the sun began to dip in earnest above the western horizon; when supper was over and, tired from weeding in the garden or washing dishes in the kitchen, she'd climb up high in her favorite apple tree, or up on a certain solid fence post, where she could see...see right into the fiery eye of the dying day. Clouds, torn remnants of noon's fat white puffs, rushed to their end in great swaths of purple, pink, and lavender, all speared through on shafts of burnished gold... She watched, and seemed to feel, each night on her perch, that she could not possibly take any more beauty; it was too much. And when she grew up, and went away to learn about life and become the woman she is now, she read the only words she'd ever find to say what she felt in a lovely line from Thornton Wilder's play Our Town, where Emily says, "Oh Earth, you're too wonderful for anybody to realize you!" Only a few do - and I am one.

First let me tell you a little about North Dakota. Both Dakotas derive their names from the Sioux Indians who called themselves "Dakota", meaning "friends." It is called the "Flickertail State" because ground squirrels or gophers, called flickertails, abound all over the state. The state flower is the wild rose, which likes to grow in frilly pink and white brambles along the fences and hedgerows, and the state bird is the meadow lark, whose song I can still hear in my heart, when I want to. The capitol is Bismarck, in the western part of the state; my folks lived in New Salem, not far away from Bismarck, after they left Kensal in their later years. A fact some people might not know is that North Dakota is the sight of one of the world's largest dams, the Garrison Dam on the Missouri River, in Garrison, just south of Minot, which was completed in 1954, a great boon to farmers. In fact, Lake Sakakawea was formed by waters held back by the dam. Sakakawea, if you'll remember your history, was the young Indian woman who led Lewis and Clark in their trek westward to the Pacific coast. North Dakota also boasts quite a line of famous native sons and daughters, many of Scandinavian descent: Lawrence Welk, Peggy Lee, Eric Severied, Roger Maris, and Angie Dickinson, to name a few.

But back to the farms. The plains didn't seem to retain water well, especially during a dry season, and there were plenty of those during the thirties. In fact, the hottest temperature ever recorded in North Dakota was in 1936 when the thermometer hit 121 degrees, and the coldest temperature ever recorded was also in that year, at 60 degrees below zero! Needless to say, the climate was not always friendly. In the old days, the farmers had to plow the land under to help it hold moisture. Still, then and now, North Dakota produces enormous amounts of grains and other foods not only for America, but for people all over the world. Some call the prairie states "The Breadbasket of the World"; and they are absolutely right!

North Dakota was also known for other attractions besides grain. For a time we lived in the Red River Valley, where the best potatoes are grown. In fact, a friend, Barbara Habels' father developed the Australian potato-harvesting equipment which he later sold to local farmers. Another friend, Harvey Beffa, (V.P. and member of the Board of Falstaff who headed the Malting Division out of Chicago) tells me he used to go to North Dakota to buy the best barley in the country, for the making of Falstaff beer in a brewery here in St. Louis. He says the soil producing the best barley is "cleaned" by planting potatoes or beets the season before. This provides the low nitrogen and protein mixture to produce the purest barley with the germination power of 90% required by Falstaff. Even today, Busch brewery has huge grain bins in Sutton, North Dakota – just a few miles from all our relatives' farms. These bins store the barley for their beer made here in St. Louis.

We all knew that life in Binford, where Dad had inherited some land, would not be easy; but I don't think either of my parents were prepared for just how difficult it would be. After all, it was 1937, and the hard times of the Depression had only just begun to fade. Nobody we knew had much money, and preachers usually had less, since few congregations had extra cash to support one. So Dad's idea was that we'd go down to Binford, where Uncle John and Uncle Mike and their vast families had been farming fairly successfully for some years. Dad's acreage bordered Uncle John's place, and this was as close as I ever got to living on a real farm.

Key to this relocation, of course, was the assumption that Dad's inheritance was farmable - which it wasn't, as we were to learn later. The fields were there, all right, but packed with rocks, left over from the last glacier centuries ago, so many that farm implements would be damaged if someone attempted to disk or plow. Well, then Dad tried to pull the rocks out, gather them up and haul them out of the field, and of course we little kids helped. We picked, and we dug and we hauled - and it wasn't long before Dad realized he just couldn't make it work. What little land he managed to clear just wasn't enough to farm and turn a profit. (You can still see those piles of rocks along the sides of the fields and sometimes in the very middle piled high.) So he turned to teaching part time, in the little school just a half mile down a two track dirt road over a culvert and through a field.

Rocks were actually a big part of our lives then, for good and ill. Uncle John had a gravel pit on one of his sections, and Dad was a frequent visitor because roads in and out of our place were terrible - just muddy troughs most of the time. So Dad and his brothers would bring out loads of gravel to try and fill in the ruts so we could drive on it. But winter weather and spring thaws were more than a match for our car, which sank up to its axles in mud with great regularity. This meant that everybody who was old enough had to get out and push the car. Sometimes we could not push it out no matter what, and then Dad would get Uncle John and his team of big horses to pull us out. Usually this was difficult even for the horses, who would strain and pull as hard as they could, but even the lash of the whip couldn't give them any more strength. I can remember these poor horses struggling so hard...I was very impressed with their bigness, their loyalty and their gentleness.

Living in the country taught me to respect animals for all they were and did for us. I can remember watching my cousins milk the cows, who'd swing and switch their tails at flies while they were being milked. I recall a cousin very frustrated trying to milk this one cow, and "accidentally on purpose" hit the cow along the back side with the three legged milking stool. Well! With that, the cow plopped her rear leg into the bucket of fresh milk! There were other times, when the cow obliged us by allowing her teat to be twisted so we could get a squirt of fresh warm milk straight from the source - or we'd watch one of the barn cats wait patiently until she too would get a squirt. I don't think any of the cats had names like the dogs did; they were always around though, lots of them, and were valued as trusty officers of rodent control.

When I got older I was assigned to gather the eggs from our resident chickens. At first it was kind of scary because these hens were sitting there on a big nest of eggs and I was not about to reach my hand down under there and make them mad by stealing their creations! But Dad and Hazel showed me how to do it with as little fuss as possible. Eventually I made up my own technique, which worked pretty well. I'd simply chase them off their nests and while they made their fuss, I grabbed the eggs and made out of there with a basket full of them as fast as I could!

But I was not safe yet. In those days, every farm had a turkey gobbler, and occasionally we did too. This big old turkey guy would make a lot of racket and strut around in a pompous goose step like he owned the place. And he did! The gobblers I knew usually hung out around the chicken coop where they paraded around sputtering every foul turkey-word they knew, no doubt; like little boys at school who cussed behind the barn just to prove they could. And the arrogance! Preening and posing, fanning his dusty brown tail feathers out like he was some hunk of a guy, and we were all supposed to be so terribly impressed. Well, I was impressed; or rather, I was terrified, for gobblers would chase anyone they sensed was afraid - and I always was! Once at Cousin Hazel's I crept out of the coop very quietly, very slowly so as not to rouse the gobbler. But he saw me, and for one split second we sized each other up; it was he or I. And he decided it was going to be me. I had to run for my life across the yard and up the wind mill to escape! I screamed and screamed, and Hazel, fearless and determined, chased the old bird away with a broom, while I climbed down and fled with my eggs in hand, my pride in shreds.

Even though I didn't live on a real farm, I was enthralled with farming - the magnitude of effort the land demanded if it was to yield us our bread. I liked watching the men work at planting and harvest time, and I envied (but not too much!) my girl cousins who were allowed to help them. My cousin Phyllis was about my age but she was also tall and big boned, as strong as the horses she loved so much. She used to tell me about how proud she was to work in the fields with the men; she was only fourteen when they decided she could. She'd get up at 5:30 a.m., go out to feed and harness the horses - and then she'd cut hay and rake it into rows. She told me how one day she stayed out in the field until she was so hungry she couldn't stand it anymore, and she walked back to the house to find the noon meal over, the kitchen empty. They'd forgotten to call her to dinner! She made a sandwich from the leftovers and went back to work, but the memory remained for years.

Poor Phyllis...like me, she was a frustrated tomboy, but she took it harder I think, because she was strong as any man so a lot of people didn't appreciate her abilities. I talk with Phyllis now and realize that "there but for the grace of God" I could have gone, had I not had more enlightened parents. I too hated household chores, hated shelling peas and setting tables; would much rather have been outside. But we all, including Bob, learned to do them right along side both Mother and Dad.

"Much rather have been cleaning out the barn, or currying the horses," Phyllis says to this day. "Gosh, I loved those horses; they were so big and beautiful...rode them whenever I could, and never used a saddle; didn't know what it was. I was just born in the wrong time, I guess. Back then women were raised to be submissive; to be refined meant a girl was "chaste" in spirit as well as fact, and devoid of any sign of cheapness, like make-up and lipstick. I wanted to wear lipstick and my mother threw a fit. So I bought a red pencil and applied it very inexpertly in the girls' bathroom at school. Then I'd wash it off before I went home! Now that I think about it, I realize it wasn't the lipstick I wanted so much as the act of rebellion....I didn't want to be a girl - not that kind of girl, anyway. In fact, it was I who introduced Rose Marie to the joys of smoking, up in my bedroom. It just about choked her; she's never smoked since, either. (Phyllis ended up marrying very young and raising a big family - much as her mother and sisters had before her.)

By the time we'd gone to live in Kensal in 1945, I was old enough to be a "hired girl" for the summer, and I looked forward to those days. I remember my first summer with Cousin Ken and Cousin Hazel; I must have been about 13 or 14. Hazel did all the cooking and baking, but I assisted right along with her, and then tended their kids, who were still little. She was an able and patient teacher, and though I must have deserved it at least once, she was never harsh or scolding with me. I always knew just what to do. I did a lot of the dishwashing, the bedmaking, the gardening...and then of course, I kept watch over the children, who were always scurrying about. Mundane chores, yes, but I enjoyed them because I could be outside a lot. Hazel moved her washing machine outside under a wonderful old shade tree right beside the clothes line, so laundry was almost a joy. (I can still hear that old ringer washer's motor.) A note of interesting tradition – Hazel still wears a dress and apron to this day.

I cleaned the separator by the north side of the house, in the shade. Have you ever seen a separator? It was a contraption designed with fifty disks that looked like little funnels, all on a rod. It separated the cream from the milk, so eventually butter could be made. We had a large wooden churn, but some of our relatives had huge wooden barrel-type churns which could handle a gallon or two of cream. We'd rotate the barrel for some time, anywhere from fifteen to forty-five minutes, depending on the freshness of the cream and the size of the container. We always liked to hear the butter rolling around inside, because then

51

we knew we were almost finished. Mother would use her wooden butter paddle to scoop the butter out of the churn, salt it a little to taste, and then mold it into small bricks for family use, or to sell in town. Nothing tasted better than fresh butter on fresh bread which Mother made so laboriously every week. Cleaning the separator was a pain because the cream got caught up in all the tiny places that were hard to reach. I had to clean them twice a day, of course - because they milked the cows twice a day.

My summer work at Hazel's was my first insight into what real farming was like at its most fevered pitch, haying and threshing time. The farmers would all help each other - they had to; every farmer needed the help of every strong back in the area to get his crop in.

In those days most harvesting was done with horse-drawn binders, each using a three or four horse hitch. In a good crop year, there would be lots of shocks to set up and a farmer would hire any strong back that came along. But in the dry thirties most crop years produced only thin, short crops nearly choked by the Russian thistle. I well remember the men having to stop the machinery to untangle the binder bundle apparatus of this hardy weed, which could stop the bull wheel on the binder when it kicked the bundle out. When the sickle, the reel, the three canvasses and the bundle started to kick out thorns, the driver had to stop everything to get off and cut twine on the bundle and pull the thistle out.

The crops - wheat, rye, oats and barley, were cut and tied into bundles by the binder. Then the bundles were picked up and stood up into shocks - ten bundles to a shock - and left there until they were dry, perhaps a couple of days. Bob and I liked to shock, and got pretty good at it, though it was tiring work. When they were dry, the threshing rig was then set up; it consisted of the tractor which was hooked to the threshing machine by a huge fan belt, which gave the thresher the power to run the bundles through. Then several flat-bed wagons called hay racks went to work; each was worked by two or three men who pitched the shocks up onto the rack. You'd see three or four racks working a single field. When the rack was full, they'd drive it over to the thresher, where the bundles were tossed onto the feeder. They kept feeding the bundles until their rack was empty - then they'd go back to the field to collect more until all the shocks were gone. On a good day, with plenty of men to work, there would be a line of racks waiting their turn at the thresher.

The bundles on the feeder would then go through the thresher, which separated the grain from the chaff (straw). The grain would come flying out into a waiting grain wagon (or truck), and the straw would fly out another pipe, making a huge pile - sometimes about two stories high. The straw was later used for bedding the animals. When the hay was cut, it was picked up by a huge rake driven by horses, and then put into rows which were later picked up with pitch forks, put into the rack and taken to the large second story of the barn, called a hay mow. This was used all winter to feed the animals, but more importantly, it was for playing in. We kids loved nothing better than to swing across the barn on a pulley rope and jump into the huge drifts of sweet hay. There was nothing so exhilarating!

Another thing we <u>loved</u> to do was to ride up on top of the hayrack. At that time, most of the farmers used horses to provide them with their needed energy. It would be a few years yet before tractors became sophisticated enough to retire horses from heavy labor. And then too, the modern combine came along. But the big thrill in those days was to see the huge steam engine pull the threshing machine into a field ripe with a full crop. Later, when the stalks of corn or barley or whatever had dried to a certain point, then they'd rake that up and put in storage in the silo - hence the word silage - which was used as winter feed for animals.

Some years earlier, farmers had their granaries cleaned out and ready for the newly mended sacks of grain, which was sacked at the machine and hauled home by horse drawn wagons and emptied into the farmer's bins. They liked to watch the sacks fill as the thresher, whirling with all manner of wheels and belts, spit out straw into a pile that kept getting bigger and bigger; piles like we'd all ski and slide down covered with snow in winter.

The farmers got really nervous when forecasts called for rain during harvest time; a good rain at the wrong time could kill an entire crop. So when the thunderclouds approached, <u>everybody</u> pitched in and worked fiendishly to get it in. Ironic, isn't it, about rain? Rain at harvest was the worst thing that could happen to a farmer; but lack of rain in spring and summer could ruin him too. When the clouds deepened, I could feel the tension in the men, and the women too. They all knew they could not - simply <u>could not</u> -lose this crop, so in a sense it was a sort of life and death matter. I don't know what they did to keep level headed about it; maybe they prayed, maybe it was the snuff they packed in their cheeks...but they usually got it in, and everyone was relieved.

Until the grasshoppers came along. Oh, you wouldn't <u>believe</u> how these insects could utterly devastate a crop - in literally nothing flat, especially in those Depression years of meager crops. They would come by the millions in massive clouds which could darken the sun; old time farmers who'd been around a while loved to tell grasshopper stories. They could move through a field in a sort of leap-frog wave of destruction. The first wave gave way to another behind it - until the field was stripped bare. They ate <u>everything</u> that wasn't nailed down, even clothing and wooden tools. I remember hearing adults talk about how some farmers would try to catch them with elaborate arrangements of canvas on a binder. Hauled by two horses, the machine could trap a good number of them which they dumped in a ditch where they were drenched in gasoline and burned. The stench, my elders said, was nearly unbearable, the operation usually futile; there were just too many of them. Horses' heads had to be protected with nose bags over their faces. Those poor animals; they faced a lean winter of meager feed, for the crops were necessary for their own survival as well as the farmer's income. Such sinister things, those hoppers. I can remember vividly walking through a field and having myriads of them flying up in my face; they took my breath away, and scared me.

Just talking about the anxiety of the harvest makes me realize just how much farmers depended upon God and whatever fates there may be for the right weather at the right time. A frost in late spring; a cyclone in June, a hail storm in July, and drought anytime, spelled ruin, or at least severe setbacks. I remember Uncle John lost two barns; one to fire, the other to a cyclone. And then of course there were those fierce winds that only the prairies know... And in the thirties, they knew them as those ceaseless Dust Bowl gales. We'd have tremendous electrical storms in the summer too, when the dry wind-scraped fields could produce just the right conditions for lots of thunder and lightening. I was terrified of these storms, and remember one incident in particular. One night we were having a real noisy buster of a storm, and I was cowering as usual. Presently I looked outside to see my father going outside and crossing the yard to the barn. And I thought, he's going to quiet the storm; he will make it stop doing this and I will be safe. That was my dad...fearless and strong, as well as kind.

Oh, the meals! Hazel fixed wonderful dishes and I know I learned a lot from her; but mostly I remember peeling potatoes. Of course in the country, the noon meal was the largest, and always called "dinner." The men would come in from the fields soaked through with sweat and grime. Hazel would put a lot of old towels out by the pump, along with a bar of felsnaptha soap; the men washed up and crowded inside, or else ate at long tables set up outside in the shade.

There was lots of mashed potatoes and gravy, some kind of meat, usually butchered right on the farm, and home grown vegetables. There were hearty stews, steaming chops, and of course, the country staple, chicken, stewed or fried. And then pies or cakes you would willingly die for. Feeding twelve or more hungry men was no small task, and Hazel worked at it most of the morning during harvest time. Then there was late afternoon snack time too. We'd make lots of sandwiches (cold meats and cheese) and carry them out to the men in a big basket, with some lemonade. I never saw anyone drink beer or anything alcoholic - I suspect there was an unspoken code between the boss and all the hands: drink, and you're out. Alcohol diminished awareness and caution, and there was no time for accidents, especially with the tricky reaper. (One cousin did get his foot chewed up in the thresher, and limped the rest of his life.)

Supper was a much lighter meal, usually from dinner's left overs or a casserole. After supper (and often after dinner) while I was helping with the dishes, the men would gather on the front porch, or out under a shade tree, where they'd discuss the weather, what machine had broken down most recently and who was fixing it, local politics, etc.

They would sit around and pick their teeth, or take a bit of snuff, pronounced "snoose" by most. Picking your teeth was bad enough, but the snuff - it was the most disgusting habit ever - and still is! ! They'd pull off a good sized chew of it, stuff it in their cheeks, suck on it for hours then spit it out. (And kept the little can of it handy in their overall pockets. In fact, the overalls had small pockets especially stitched to hold the snuff cans - directly over their hearts!) My father used some on occasion, but he always got rid of it outside. Most men let it rip inside, and their wives had to keep special spittoons around the house for them to spit it out. (Hazel, I might add, never allowed a spittoon in the house.) I'll never forget the trip I made back there in 1985, when my mother and Dorothy and I flew up there for Dad's funeral. The man who met us at the plane spat the stuff into a coffee can on the dashboard, in between swigs of something from a jug slung over his shoulder!

Until World War Two was well underway, times were hard for farmers - and hence everyone else in country towns. Families suffered a lot, and in more ways than financial. We knew of a woman who married a man who became alcoholic, and when he was drunk, she and the children suffered; they were so poor.

Perhaps the most pathetic victims of all in those dark days, were, as I've said, the wandering men we called bums, who were just tramps. Some had always been drifters, a good many others had families at one time, and lost them when they lost their jobs; a wife might take the children and go back to live with her family if her wayward spouse couldn't get work. They "rode the rails" (hitched rides by jumping in empty box cars of moving trains) all over the country. They'd stay somewhere and work for some farmer at harvest, or at other odd jobs, just long enough to earn money to tide them over for a while. They'd sleep in a cheap hotel room, or in a farmer's barn, grab a few good meals, and then they were off again to the next town. They came often enough to beg work of the farmers I knew, and their help at harvest was always welcome. They'd work as long as they were needed - were given good meals and a place to sleep in the barn. Many weren't very reliable. They'd agree to work two weeks, and after five days they'd be gone, no explanation - just vanished with the night. The farmer might then have to go to the nearest employment agency in town and try to find another hand - always frustrating at busy times. My Uncle John often hired seminary students from St. Louis who were generally reliable and certainly needed the money.

While the Depression affected everyone, none of us children really understood just how hard life was for most people (probably because we were young and had nothing to compare our lives with). But many people, especially the men, suffered badly. With the massive breakdown of the national economy, millions of men were simply laid off from their jobs. Whole industries dried up over night.

It wasn't until 1933, when Franklin D. Roosevelt became president that anything began to crack the sense of defeat and hopelessness of an entire country. Roosevelt initiated a number of national work projects, the most notable being the Works Projects Administration (WPA), which employed thousands of poor and jobless men. Teams of these men were trained and then sent to work to build everything from roads and highways, dams, to municipal buildings. A good many were even employed building and maintaining day care centers for the children of women who, by 1942, flocked to the factories to take the jobs left by the men who went to war. Similar to the WPA, was the CCC, Civilian Conservation Corps, which also furnished training and work for young men in the process of conserving our natural resources of water, timber and soil. I can remember hearing about trees being planted, parks being created, forest fires contained, all by the CCC. Another off shoot of the WPA was the NYA, the National Youth Administration, who employed young people in similar public projects. Some of these proved invaluable labor forces when the country went to war. But despite all these efforts, many people still suffered, particularly the farmers.

Despite hard times, cruel fate and a sometimes inexplicable God, the farmers I knew all loved their work. Even today, you'll find the same land being farmed by the 4th or 5th generation of the same family. There's an old saying that goes, "You have to do what you love." For these people, farming is all there is - it is in them, like marrow in the bone, and pride in the heart. Farming is their life, and the land is their song.

Chapter Four

"Let It Snow, Let It Snow, Let It Snow...."

As if we could stop it! North Dakota winter came early and all in a rush; no gentle transition from autumn's crisp nip to Jack Frost's fierce grip. No, it was usually a great woosh of frigid north wind that swept in off the prairies like a freight train bound for glory. It seemed like one morning we woke up to a gale we knew meant business, and we'd watch the sky all day in school, knowing that soon, soon…maybe tonight it would come, the magic…We'd go to bed that first blustery night listening to the whole house shiver and every window rattle. When we woke up the next morning we <u>knew</u>, because it was so quiet, that it had come - the first eiderdown blanket of the winter, soft and muted but not without a sense of humor. Who else would think to top the old stumps and fence posts with conical snow caps?!

In a few months we knew we'd be sick of the snow, but in those first few winter weeks, we kids were all enchanted. When we'd have three day blizzards (not uncommon), we'd literally be snowed in our house for days. And the drifts! The wind would blow so hard your door would be blocked. You'd open your door and face a wall of snow, as high as the house sometimes. That's why farmers would string ropes at about 4 feet high from the house to the barn so they could find their way through the drifts to feed the animals. Since the temperature stayed well below freezing for weeks at a time, the snow never melted. Each successive snow fall simply piled up higher.

To us children, the snow was the most wonderful playmate. We'd all clamor to go outside as soon as possible - which took some doing because we had to put on several layers of clothing. A Dakota winter's below-zero temperatures could be dangerous, so we learned to take care when we were very young. We'd start with our long white winter underwear, maybe a couple of sweaters, and then the heavy snow suit, complete with hood. It's amusing to me to remember that in those days, in a land of long, cold months, little girls were still expected to wear dresses to school. No matter how bitter the cold, no matter how deep the snow, we still had to show up at school in dresses. What a chore it was to stuff your skirt down into the two legs of your snowsuit! If there wasn't any snow, but it was bitter cold, we wore our play pants under our dresses and wool coats, and then had to take them off in school, which was, as I've said, never warm enough! Lastly the wool scarf Mother wrapped around our faces all the way up to our eyes. We often helped each other with the knot in the back; naturally we would pull it extra tight if we felt in a teasing mood. The recipient, though, didn't always take the gesture as a tease - and might bop you one! I felt the scarf was a nuisance; it would get so wet and warm from breathing through it that, in the freezing temperatures, my eye lashes and brows frosted over so I looked like a gnome from the North Pole.

Like most who live in North Dakota, we were friends with winter - to us it was a great big bumbling playmate and we loved to play with it, or better, in it. One of the best winter play feats was sliding down snow covered haystacks or strawstacks. We'd hit bottom with such speed that we kept right on gliding over the hard snow for another eighth of a mile! We had only one sled, so of course we had to take turns, two of us on it at once. Great fun, even though we had to walk the long way back. And of course the higher the haystack the better the ride. Sometimes when we had a deep snow, we could slide down the roof of the chicken coop or the garage roof. Sometimes the fierce winds would bank into huge drifts; and it was so hard and high we could walk over the ground to the pitch of the garage roof. We felt like kings and played a game called "King of the Hill" - almost as good as the view from the boxcars!

We also made large snow caves, which we dug out with our hands and shovels (hence the frequent need for new mittens); sometimes we formed blocks with which we built igloos. I recall playing "store" in those igloos, complete with cardboard money and shelves of "canned" goods - provisions for local trappers and eskimos, you understand. We made snow forts and staged snowball fights. If we had a heavy spring snow, we'd hide our Easter eggs in the snow!

We had one pair of skis and one sled to share among the five of us so we made deals as to who got what when. Improvising was just a fact of our life, so we were always commandeering boxes, pieces of wood and metal, anything we could fashion into some sort of snow play gear.

Of course we rolled around in the fluffy stuff...had to make our quota of "angels" and snowmen on the ground, and play endless games of Fox and Geese. On Saturdays when we had lots of time, we'd burrow into snow drifts to make tunnels and caves. We'd get so excited that we hardly felt cold. As long as we could keep moving we could bear the cold; sometimes we stayed out for two hours at a stretch. Eventually the fingers and toes would begin to burn with tension and pain. By the time we'd brushed each other off with the broom, we'd be crying with the sting of frozen mittens, scarf, snow suit. Mother and Dad would help us take it all off, especially our clumsy snow boots, always a chore to get on and off. Then we'd sit on the furnace register, when we had one; or we'd stand around the hot kitchen stove.

A Dakota snow fall was not always so playful; it could be deadly too. Mom, Dad and Tudy nearly died once when a blizzard crept right up on them. They'd been visiting Reverend Mehls in Wimbledon, and didn't leave until after dark, so the sky gave them no warning. It just began to snow furiously until Dad could not see to drive, and the car simply could not function in the swirls and folds of wind-driven white. Eventually they got stuck in a snow bank, so they had to get out and make their way back to Wimbledon. Mom said she was so cold and wet she'd have willingly just died there in a snowbank, but Dad literally carried her and Tudy for miles back to town.

You can bet we heard that story over and over again. Mom kept reminding us that many a person has frozen to death in a very short time in a snowbank due to exhaustion. One could become unconscious very quickly and freeze stiff in no time, she always said. (She wanted to make sure we never went out and did something foolish like that.) We heard about frostbite too, how you could lose fingers and toes and ears and nose. You know how kids are - we'd scare each other with tales of how your skin turned white, and when it thawed out you'd cry with the most incredible pain and then your nose would fall off...we all had our stories!

The snow will always be a glorious gift for me. How I loved to wake up to a bright, sun-dazzling morning after a new snowfall. The wind had hardened the surface, so when we looked out we'd see acre after acre of sun-cut diamonds for as far as we could see. I loved to walk on it, hear the hard crunch of my feet sinking into its brilliance...that's one of my most cherished childhood memories.

But the snow's sunny songs didn't end at sundown; it simply transposed its glories into another key - and wrote them across the night. After a good snow, even the night sky would be exceptionally clear, and the air so bright and crisp that I could almost hear it "ping" like a crystal goblet when you flick a finger on the rim. It would be so bright out, with the snow reflecting the moon's light...everything was bathed in a romantic glow. As kids we invented night time games to play in the white. But even though I was just a child I felt something like reverence for it; I used to bundle up and go out just to see the moon, never more brilliant but ethereal too, its corona reaching out for the Northern Lights. Mom and Dad taught us how to find the Big and Little Dippers, and Orion, and when a star shot across the heavens, we all felt humbled by the glories God had made for us. A family tradition was, that if you said "Money, money, money!" three times when you saw a shooting star, you'd get rich. We never did, though we chanted to enough shooting stars; but we didn't care. We thought we were rich enough in other things, so we thanked the Lord for His natural wonders, for strength, courage and faith He gave us to go through life.

I will never forget the night after we buried Dad in January of 1985, in his beloved North Dakota. I left the company of family and friends to slip on a coat and step outside Ken and Hazel's house where we were staying, to see the snow and the moon - and it was glorious! The glistening snowy fields stretched around me, endless, infinite, while the cold silver light of the moon blessed and comforted me. In that moment I knew, as I've never known before, that God lives, that He loves us; that life is good, that death is simply a transformation of natural states, just as snow is only water in another form. I stood there, quiet, praying; I didn't want it to end. Then like a child again, I came running inside and announced to everyone (all playing cards, of course) that we were blessed with the most wonderful "glow" on that sad night, and they must all come outside and see it. I grabbed Mother's wraps and gently covered her, and led her and Dorothy outside to stand with me in the moonlight. There in that white night, we shared quiet, tearful moments together, and were comforted. I feel sure Dad knew we were there. As did our Heavenly Father, for surely that is why he gives us such miracles, and such moments to realize them. My faith in Him grows with every year. He gave me wonderful parents, family, relatives and friends whom I love and depend upon daily for the courage and strength I need for day to day living. Nothing counts more than that...there is nothing more.

Dad Leininger graduation
from college in St. Paul, Minn.

Walter Edwin Leininger
Concordia Seminary Graduation 1923

Helen Rose Behrmann
High School Graduation 1925

Cousin Phyllis's birthday party in the country
BINFORD 1939

Rose Marie • Lois • Dorothy
BINFORD 1933

Mountains of Snow
DEEP, North Dakota 1939

Mountains of Snow
DEEP, North Dakota 1939

Our Family
1943

Our Family
1946

Folks House 1954
ISLAND GROVE, Illinois
Where Walt and I were married

DEEP, North Dakota
1939-1945

Our Family
1948

Our Home in KENSAL (1945)
1945-1952

Dorothy • Bob • Rose Marie
Lois • Estelle

Dad and Mom

At Camp
Lois • Dorothy • Rose Marie

Rose Marie Leininger
Registered Nurse 1954

Rose Marie Leininger
High School Graduation 1949

Chapter Five

*"The More We Get Together, Together, Together,
The More We Get Together, the Happier We'll Be...."*

Church and family gatherings stood at the core of any rural North Dakota community, and our extended family, being so big, never lacked for an occasion to get together. Somebody was always having a birthday or an anniversary and so we all descended upon the house of the Birthday Boy/Girl like a cloud of grasshoppers for a big celebration. Sometimes we got together for no reason at all than to see each other - and eat and talk! So there was a lot of traveling between us; in North Dakota, people didn't come to see us, as much as we went to see them.

I know many towns had special Fourth of July events, complete with community band and a parade, but I don't recall ever going to such a thing. We always got together with family and would frequently meet in the same grove of trees on somebody's farm. Some of them came from a good distance away in their well worn cars or trucks over miles of rutted dirt roads. Dusty but excited, everyone arrived in a jubilant mood, ready for a celebration. Of course everyone brought a huge picnic, which the women spread out on long tables made from sawhorses and wooden planks. Oh, you would not believe the food! The women had all prepared their best casseroles, cold chickens and hams, baked beans, potato salads, pickles, home baked bread, pies, cakes and even a few ethnic dishes. After the feast, we'd play croquet, very popular and very competitive with the Leiningers, and the adults would play cards later. As dusk settled in, we kids were allowed to light some minor fireworks like "sparklers" with the help of an adult; always we were reminded of how very dangerous firecrackers could be.

When we lived in Binford and Kensal, birthdays were a BIG DEAL. Every Leininger within fifty miles would drive over and show up at the birthday house door. "Where's the party!?" I do remember all the folks coming over to our place, but mostly I remember driving to other Leininger houses because they had so many more birthdays than we did with only seven people. I loved visiting our farm cousins, because then I could ride the cows and calves (much more accessible than horses, and less fearsome,) or play in the barn. I do remember one wild horseback ride with my cousin Phyllis, who knew and loved the big draft horses her dad kept to pull wagons. The idea was that we'd both ride our separate horses into the fields. Well, my horse must have caught wind of the plan, because he refused to go anywhere. I reined him and, in fact, took off in the opposite direction! He must have sensed I didn't know what I was doing and he certainly took full advantage of the situation. I don't know what I'd have done if Phyllis hadn't been near. Anyway, later there'd be cake, great big slabs of it, maybe some hand cranked ice cream, and revelry until nearly midnight on occasion. Everybody loved it!

They say studies show that people who live in cold climates and have dreary days show an increased incidence of depression, even suicide. I never saw that...everyone I knew was far too busy to get depressed. In those days though, the word "depression" meant the tremendous slump in the economy we all suffered. It would be decades before doctors would give that same name to those dark periods of unhappiness and despair that plagued my mother. Then, mental illness meant the more bizarre manifestations of disturbance like schizophrenia or paranoia, and if it cropped up somewhere in the family, it was hushed and never spoken of to anyone. Those who did feel deeply unhappy rarely let on; they knew they'd be chastised by their minister as having too little faith. (Considered by Lutherans to be the root of most of life's difficulties, I might add.)

But for the most part, we were a happy bunch of people, maybe because our faith in God's care was strong enough to keep the blues away. I don't ever remember anyone in our large extended family being angry with any of the others. Maybe there were just too many of us to allow for the depth and breadth necessary for a full blown tiff. We were close to each other - an hour or two by car - but we were also just far enough apart that we didn't see each other regularly, so no one had the time or the inclination. If there were tiffs, I suspect Dad knew about them and kept them from his "preacher's kids" lest one of us might innocently let some cat out of its bag. Anyway, even today the Leiningers continue to "get together" for family reunions every five years. Last time we met in Fargo, about a two hour drive from Binford, and crowded into a city park - all 700 of us!

Christmas then was always very simple. In our Binford and Kensal years, we almost always went to one of the Leininger houses, which were about 30 miles away. In our years at Deep, nearly two hours by car in good winter weather, we stayed at home. Most of our energy went into a nice program at church in which everyone, especially the children, could participate. We kids were drilled until we could say our "piece" perfectly; the Christmas service was a very Big Deal. Mother always made sure we had a nice new Christmas dress she'd made herself, or one Grandma Behrmann sent from Indianapolis. Of course Dad had to preach on Christmas, and usually we had to go to two churches on Christmas Day, though some years Dad had to travel to others as well. (He'd fill in for fellow preachers who had to be gone for one reason or another.) Eventually though, we came home to our own little tree which we'd set up in the parlor, and decorated with our small but ever expanding collection of ornaments Mother had bought or been given, one season at a time. We never had electric lights, so we used real little candles about four inches long on our tree, which we lit for a short time on Christmas Eve. We didn't have a lot of shiny baubles, but we did have lots of tinsel which we threw on with abandon; and in the soft candle glow, our silvery little tree was the most beautiful in the world.

We'd have our gift opening after church on Christmas morning, and our presents were usually clothes and books. My mother was big on mittens, which we went through quickly, so we'd usually find a new pair for each of us under the tree. I remember we girls getting a new barrette or new ribbons for our hair, or a sweater; simple, practical. We didn't get toys, with the exception of baby dolls for the girls. Over the years in our childhood, we each got two dolls. We used to dress the baby dolls in our own baby clothes; later, when we graduated to standard "girl" dolls, Mother would patiently stitch up clothes for them, right down to their underwear! I can't imagine the patience, because this was a real undertaking for four daughters' worth of dolls! When we were older, we got a set of checkers, and then the popular new game, Monopoly - which we loved. Many a long winter weekend was spent competing in this game.

For Lutherans, "Mission Festival" was another big get-together occasion, usually held in the summer. It was a day-long affair with two very long church services, one in the morning, the other in the afternoon, wherein a "special" visiting preacher would address the congregation. Everyone was supposed to go to both services, regardless of cranky infants and restless children (or even our own boredom); but I remember many families did not stay for the afternoon service. They were tired, they'd eaten too much, they'd sweat enough, and the children irritable and whiny, so many left after the huge pot luck dinner. We, of course, had to stay to the bitter end. I can still remember sitting through those afternoon sessions fanning my face with my limp program, and watching some cute baby's face three rows up, or maybe a fly settling on some man's bald head... Such were my spiritual attentions at Mission Festivals!

The church also had a meeting for the women called "Ladies Aid." Every two weeks the church women would go to one of their homes for socializing, and a brief instructional message and bible devotional from Dad. I've often wondered how Dad got through those afternoons, being the only male present in the midst of all those women - and children and babies! Of course, we kids went along with Mom in the summer and on holidays from school, or when we were too sick to go to school. We were supposed to behave as the docile, well mannered children of a man of God - which we never were, of course. Oh, we tried. We played Drop the Handkerchief and Ring Around the Rosie (the only fun here was getting to be "it.") But it was tough going, even though these games were fun for awhile. Usually the boys broke first and fell to rough-housing; we girls must have just played paper dolls or some other benign activity.

What I remember most was getting to sit on my aunts' spacious laps. They had such nice wide bosomy laps, great for taking naps in, and I was always up for some snugly time in a lap while the women quilted or did their mending, which many brought along. The women I knew were farmers' wives and had little time for home crafted niceties. A farm and kids demanded 100% from everyone, and maybe 200% from farm women.

Of course Dad spoke. Then they'd talk over lunch, always scrumptious, especially if they had those divine pecan cinnamon rolls which I devoured as I listened silently to their musings. I think back to those meetings and realize how profoundly they influenced my life - for these women, most of them farm wives, really defined what womanhood was at that time and in that place; it was from them and my mother that I discerned just what I was destined to be in life - a handmaid, a help-mate, a nurturer. There simply was <u>nothing</u> else to be then, there. And even though I was so young, I knew even then that I'd carry on their legacy somehow - and I have.

Then too there were the periodic meetings with the various pastors in the circuit and their families. (A circuit was a geographic area designated by some elder churchmen of the synod many years ago.) We always went to one of the pastors' homes, and while the men had their study and discussion time, the women would sit around looking all prim and proper. They might have brought some hand work to do, but that didn't last long as there were squabbling kids to referee, crying babies to sooth, and the potluck meal to prepare.

After we ate, the game of choice was always cards in the winter months, and croquet in the warm ones. Sometimes the women would play but generally they didn't because they had to supervise the children or help with the dishes. Croquet was a game every child in our area learned to play from the time they could stand. I loved the competition of it and got pretty good at it if I may say so. Actually we all loved to play it, as much as we played Monopoly in the winter. And those "pious" men! You wouldn't believe how competitive they could be.

Other times we'd visit another family after church on Sunday just because we'd been "invited out" as they put it. When we lived in Deep we'd travel fifty miles over a gravel road to visit the Brauers who lived in Minot - which had a big pool! Mother always packed food for a picnic with them; and sometimes we'd stay overnight which was a BIG thrill. We got to use the Brauers' bathroom and electric lights - a great treat for us since such things were only dreamed of luxuries. I remember too being invited to my best friend Lori Hall's (now Duesenberg) farm, where I knew we were guaranteed a whole afternoon of eating and playing!

Mostly though, we visited members of the congregation who "invited us out," and this meant at least one meal, possibly two. We kids were always told to eat everything we dished up for ourselves, most especially when we were visiting another home; so we did not consider very long what to do with something we didn't like. Dislike of a food was rare and I loved it all, believe me. I've often wondered why I remained such a slip of a girl despite all those dishes lavished in cream and butter. I guess it was all the running around we did - we must have burned it off as fast as we ate it.

Food in those days had its own special etiquette. For example, my husband Don's family, fluent in German, used the word "unverschämt" in reference to extravagant helpings - in short, taking too much. Eyebrows would raise at large servings or putting too much jelly on your bread. You were shameful - while acting shameless! I remember we kids would sit as guests at a table and calculate just how much we dared take of creamed potatoes, or fried chicken. We monitored ourselves very carefully or we knew we'd feel guilty for days about taking more than our share. Food was one of the most important things in our lives; indeed, it was often the very reason for meeting, the catalyst for socializing. Nearly every event was centered around food. It kept us going and we looked forward to our "invited out" meals with great anticipation. We knew the food would be good and we wouldn't have to wash the dishes!

Most times the adults would adjourn to the parlor after the meal to play cards, whist or pinochle or hearts or sheepshead. The hours passed and it would grow late - but not too late for a "midnight lunch". To refuse was considered very impolite; after all, the hostess had whipped up some buns, cookies, bars, pies or cakes just for your entertainment. To refuse would be an insult. So we had pie or bars with coffee for the adults (no decaf then, but I never heard of anyone not sleeping at the end of a farmer's day) and what we called nectar for the kids. Nectar was a liquid concentrate which was mixed with water and sugar in a big pitcher to make what we know today as Koolade. The men were always served first, the kids last.

Then the kids, who were very tired by this time, would be shuffled off to bed, however makeshift. We were told to go upstairs to the main bedroom where all the coats were stacked. How well I remember burrowing into the folds of a coat that suited my sense of smell and texture. Falling off to sleep was real easy by then, and I slept through all the chatter and laughter downstairs. I can remember being awakened gently, or sometimes carried to the car, which Dad had usually warmed up for us. And that long, sleepy ride home...we slept through it in a dream. The worst part of the evening was the next part - getting home to a cold house and colder sheets! Then taking off all those layers of clothes in the cold air, and crawling into bed...where we slept in a peace that defied even a Dakota night's chill.

Chapter Six

"Those Jolly Old Blues..."

As you can imagine, we five kids were <u>very active</u>; in fact, "aggressive" might be a better word, maybe because of the cold climate, more likely because we were just born that way. My poor parents...we kept them busy constantly with our bruises and cuts and scrapes; one or another of us was always nursing something. And while the pain of the wound itself was unpleasant, you can bet we played to the hilt the cherished role of "The Injured One." What good was a cut if you didn't get at least a bandage over it to show off to the other kids?

Raised pretty much out in the open, we did a lot of running and jumping - and climbing through fences and up trees and around haystacks. So we did plenty of tripping and falling on our knees and elbows, or slipping down from trees, or catching an arm as we tried to climb through a barbed wire fence. (We knew how to crawl a barbed wire fence carefully, but when you're being chased by four Wild Indians, caution flies to the wind; speed is the thing in a dramatic escape.) To this day I still have five distinct scars on my legs and knee caps, trophies from my childhood tom boy days. I look at them now, fifty years later, and remember the occasion of nearly every one with a smile.

Once the drama had subsided, it was inside to Mother and the medicine chest to face the music. In those days everyone took care of their own wounds at home. Doctors were scarce, and many miles away, so their counsel was sought only in serious emergencies. Most families made do with minor mishaps. Mother would scrub - and I do mean <u>scrub</u> the open wound with a <u>brush</u> until we could hardly stand it. Then she'd top it with some sort of disinfectant like iodine or mercurochrome - even Listerine sometimes; and they all burned like He--!! Then we'd get the bandage, usually some soft gauze and tape. We hollered a lot through the whole procedure but by golly, we rarely ever got an infection.

People used home remedies a lot back then; like hot mustard plasters for lung congestion, honey mixtures for coughs. Seems like we Leiningers always had dry skin, and skin that was susceptible to skin irritations. I remember my father always rubbing Resinol into the palm of his left hand. For some reason, that hand itched and burned a lot, and he never really got rid of it. A couple of his brothers and our cousins also had itching problems, and they'd often share some new salve they'd tried recently. Another big household item was Lysol, which was used then as it is today, to clean and disinfect bathroom areas, and kitchen sinks and floors.

We did have our share of minor disasters. Once Lois fell off the wood pile and broke her arm, and from the way she hollered, we all knew we'd be making a trip to the doctor. And once Dorothy slipped down a high haystack and was knocked unconscious briefly - or at least she said she didn't remember anything. I guess the most serious incident happened with Dorothy when we lived in Deep. She developed a blister on her heel during high school basketball practice and blood poisoning set in. We knew she needed more than our home remedies, and took her to the Catholic hospital in Bottineau for treatment. She had to stay several weeks while they used hot packs and other things to curb the infection. We were so afraid she might die. I remember visiting her there and watching all those dour nuns with their long black robes and flapping veils. How they clanked as they walked with all those rosaries and keys on long chains. Of course, being good Lutherans, and Dad having told us about the "evils" of the Catholic Church, all this was kind of sinister - and fascinating! Secretly, I adored them, no matter what anybody said. But eventually Dorothy got well, and we were all thankful and appreciative of their work - and told them so.

Another time Dorothy fell really hard on her head while she was roller skating. Boy, were we scared! Self proclaimed as the strong one in the family, I insisted that I stay with her in the doctor's office in Jamestown while she had her stitches. Well, she was lying there on the table, talking away, she and the doctor laughing together while he stitched, and then, The Great Comforter, promptly passed out cold. The doctor was worried, and when I revealed that I'd passed out on a couple of recent occasions at church, he ordered tests. As he suspected, I was somewhat anemic. "More iron for this one!" he told my mother.

Of course since we were always visiting some relative or other for a birthday party, or an anniversary, we had plenty of opportunities to get into mischief with our many cousins. And we did, without fail. We might play hide and seek or some other organized game, but mostly we ran and jumped and climbed trees or goofed around in the barn. One time was especially memorable. A bunch of us ate a lot of green crab apples - and came down with tremendous stomach aches later! Once we were home again, we were lined up and given a "dose" (i.e. one tablespoon) of Castor Oil. YYYYYUUUUKK! This was straight stuff, undiluted, so the taste alone was nearly lethal. We'd get a slice of orange to take the edge off. Then we'd wait for nature to take its course, which it usually did. (Need I say we never again touched wild fruits we didn't know about?) Dad was always the Doser because we knew we couldn't fuss with Dad; he gave us our daily dose of cod liver oil too, one spoonful and a slice of orange. We had to take it down in a silent gulp - no complaints allowed. The medical and pharmaceutical benefits of cod liver oil have since been challenged, but back then, most children got it because it was supposed to ward off illness. And - none of us ever really got sick beyond the usual childhood diseases. Only Lois seemed to have a recurrent cough, which was later diagnosed as bronchitis; and alas, she still gets it easily today. But all of us, thank God, are relatively healthy to this day.

Like most children, we did succumb to measles - the three day rubella and the two week variety too, called hard measles or rubeola - chicken pox, mumps and whooping cough, which Tudy got to a severe degree; we were afraid she might choke to death. This was back in the days when medicine knew little about immunology and vaccines. We did know that if a child got measles, he would be immune to it later in life when the disease could have serious repercussions, such as poor eyesight. The same went for mumps, chicken pox, and whooping cough. Diphtheria, however, was different; it was a killer at any time in life, but children suffered terribly from its usually fatal grip. Other serious diseases like rheumatic fever and scarlet fever could kill a child, and at the very least impair heart muscles, even some brain functions so seriously that the child might be affected for the rest of his life.

The biggest fear among families then, though, was poliomyelitis (infantile paralysis) - "polio" - a devastating disease that wrought terrible physical havoc (often permanent) at the least, or death, which was common. Polio was an acute viral disease which attacked the central nervous system. Paralysis could occur in most muscle tissues of the body, either in limbs or organs. Atrophied muscles resulted in paralysis; in many cases the respiratory and circulatory systems were damaged to such a degree that children could no longer breathe for themselves, and so were placed in coffin-like "iron lungs" which worked their lungs for them for months, even years. Many patients could recoup some lost limb function with rigorous physical therapy, but most could not. Adults could contract the disease too, for example, our President Roosevelt while still a very young man. It was a terrible killer; the virus was thought to proliferate in crowds, and many people kept their children away from crowds for that reason. One of Dorothy's old boy friends contracted polio and died just before her wedding in 1951, a sad loss to everyone. But then, in 1955, the miracle came. Dr. Jonas Salk and Dr. Albert Sabine made one of the greatest medical breakthroughs of all time, a vaccine to prevent polio; once inoculated, you were immune to the disease for life. Within just a few years, polio vanished from the medical scene, never to return, and the fear of this particularly devastating disease crept away.

Inevitably we all managed to contract our illnesses at the same time. I remember when we all had measles, my parents had to hire a young woman to

81

help with the cooking (the endless batches of soup and Jello), laundry (we went through a lot of sheets), and dishes. (Now that part of the measles we really liked - no dishes.) But we were sick as dogs for nearly two weeks. I remember Mother pulled down the dark green shades in our room because it was thought to reduce eye damage. She also kept the windows open a few inches, and I'll never forget the way those shades banged and banged against the windows, blown by the fierce prairie winds...I almost feel sick again to think about those senseless, clamoring shades.

Other families were not so fortunate as we were in our safe passage through dangerous waters. Cousin Edith, only twenty years old, was the daughter of Uncle Mike and Aunt Clara; she contracted osteomyelitis, an inflammation of the bones caused by a staphylococcus bacteria which also crippled. She needed extensive medical treatment for a long time, which involved scraping (debriding) the bones of her legs to rid them of the debris caused by the continuous, persistent infection. She had the disease very badly, and I remember the family talking often about her - she was so pretty, and in such pain. She was never able to marry. Ironically an English doctor, Alexander Fleming, had discovered penicillin in 1929, a medicine which was later used widely for many killer bacterial diseases. However, the substance was not perfected for use until 1941, and it was its extensive but still experimental use during the war in treatment of wounded soldiers that made the drug readily available after 1945. I do remember though that the doctor was able to have some of this miraculous new drug flown in especially for Edith, as she was in such terrible pain.

Another disease everyone feared was tuberculosis, also referred to as "TB" or, in Europe where it was prevalent and a common cause of death, "consumption." Caused by a bacteria which infected the lungs, TB was considered communicable through coughing the germ into the air. The only cure known was rest, sunshine and preferably life in a dry, warm climate. (That's why so many northern Europeans went to hostels in Italy and southern Spain - the climate was thought to be conducive to healing.) By the early twentieth century, victims were carefully isolated from the general public in sanatoriums developed just for the treatment of TB. I remember hearing as a child, about people (sometimes whole families) who were taken away from their relatives and put in these institutions until they got better (which might take two years) - or died. Death was not uncommon.

By now you can begin to understand how treacherous childhood could be before modern medicines came along with drugs and vaccines. Now, most childhood diseases have vanished (if the children are inoculated); small pox is said to be extinct world wide now, thanks to vaccines. Until the post-war period, parents still worried over any disease their children might contract, because they could and did wipe out entire families of children within days. My father was called upon a number of times to bury a child, sometime two or three, who'd died of diphtheria. I can vaguely remember sitting in our car as Dad walked across a dreary cemetery to say final words of comfort to a grieving family who'd just lost a child or two. In many cases, funerals were small or skipped entirely, because people feared to be out and about with a contagious disease lurking in the midst of the community. Certainly children were kept indoors whenever possible. I well remember Dad officiating in the pouring rain at the burial of my best friend Lori Hall Duesenberg's brother, who had died of diphtheria. So you see, we fearless five were very lucky indeed to have been so healthy then, and into our adult lives.

I've referred to Dad's stomach problems several times, so perhaps this is a good time to explain the final diagnosis of diabetes some years later. After another bout of symptoms, Dad decided to go many miles and hours to the hospital in Fargo. (If you had major problems, you went to Fargo.) Mother took the train and met him there, so they could both learn about the diet, the difficult balance between calories and carbohydrates and fats, to keep the body from making too much sugar, or on the other hand, to prevent too little, which would result in an insulin reaction.

Since you're probably wondering what we all looked like, I'll digress a bit here and tell you. Mother and Dad were both tall and slim, so we took after them in general physical make-up. Dorothy and I were tallest of the girls for a long time and to this day have stayed pretty slim. Tudy had more trouble with her weight until, at age 45, she turned up with diabetes; since then she's trimmed down, so the four of us still look pretty good considering our ages. Bob was like Dad, tall and muscular, and as I look back, it was no small accomplishment that the tomboy Rose Marie was able to keep up with him in all our childhood high jinxs. He was and still is strong - and while I may not be able to chin up to the bar as well anymore, I'd still take him on in an arm wrestle any day!

As photos will indicate, I was a scrawny little kid, wiry and quick, "boyish" I liked to think. But I did have to have glasses at an early age (due to astigmatism) - which I abhorred!! Glasses??? But they were so ugly! And definitely un-boyish. I despaired, but there was no getting around them - I knew I needed them and I wore them, but felt very embarrassed too. My first ones were wire rimmed and made me look like an old hag, I thought. But I wore them as directed and eventually I didn't need them anymore - or maybe I just plain decided that I'd had enough of being ugly, thank you.

My front teeth were separated too, a condition I didn't pay much mind to when I was little, but did as I grew into adolescence and began to connect boys with appearance. My folks tell me that I fell off a table when I was a toddler and the fall killed a certain nerve in my front tooth. Dad always joked that I had air conditioned teeth. I remember trying very hard not to smile so as to show my teeth, but to just clench my lips and turn up the corners, or cover my mouth. You can have no idea how the spaces between my four front teeth affected my socialization and self esteem during my teen years. When I got older I was able to have some dental work done which corrected the problem, but not until I was 19 and well into nurses' training. The day I had my new artificial front tooth placed in that space, was the happiest day of my life. Better late than never! I've enjoyed smiling ever since, believe me.

Chapter Seven

"Readin' and 'Ritin' and 'Rithmetic,
Done to the Tune of the Hickory Stick..."

The old nursery rhyme "Ring Around the Rosie, Pockets Full of Posies" comes to mind when I think of my childhood. For that's exactly what I have now, pockets in my mind full of happy childish playtime memories that bloom up as fresh and fragrant as any of my Dad's beautiful summer flowers. No matter how dreary the day, I can always slip my hand down into the past and bring forth some summer day's water fight, some winter day's snow fort, each ready to blossom at a moment's soft touch.

It's probably no surprise that, being so financially strapped during the thirties and early forties, we had few toys and had to invent our own entertainments - or perhaps we were <u>able</u> to invent our own, and thus stimulate our already wild imaginations. We girls did have some dolls, and if we wanted something else, like a toy gun to play war with, we made it ourselves from pieces of scrap lumber. If we wanted to stage a sea battle, or a pleasure cruise, we made our own boats out of wood and nails and floated them in the ditches along the sides of the roads.

Basically, we just had a great time playing with each other. My parents were too busy to play with us, and we really didn't need anyone else. I hear a lot about how today's parents don't have time to spend with their kids; but most parents I knew didn't have any time either, though in our family we knew they were always there for us... These people were in the vital business of working their farms, or "tending their flocks" as you might say my father did. And most housewives then were very busy just providing the basics in food, clothing and shelter - this was back in the days when hired help was nearly unheard of (used only in emergency situations like our measles), and dishwashers and vacuum cleaners and automatic washing machines were still on some drawing board in a big city, far away. Men and women have always both had "careers", though housewifery was not then (and still isn't today) recognized as a career. Only in the two decades following World War II has most of American society lived what people incorrectly refer to as the "traditional" nuclear family of working father/housewife mother in the picket-fenced house with two adorable kids standing at the gate. After my first husband, Walter, died, I had to work to support my three young boys; yet I always found time to play with them. I taught them how to play ball, took them to fencing lessons, to cub scout meetings, piano and violin lessons, and I read to them every day for years, until they were old enough to read to me. When I remarried, both Don and I continued to make time to "play" with the boys. It was important to them - and anyway, I'm still a tomboy at heart - and I still love to play!

My sisters and I played a lot with our dolls and paper dolls; we'd cut out clothes for our paper dolls we'd designed ourselves, or cut from a catalogue. We saved cardboard boxes which we made into "houses"; we'd subdivide them into floors and rooms, and we made little pieces of furniture for them. Among the four of us, we had a regular neighborhood! Eventually Dad made us a big doll house for our paper dolls, and we even had store bought furniture in it! I remember how intricate they were. But this was for our "adult" paper dolls; for our baby dolls, it was different. We had to be a little careful with these, because while their stuffed cotton bodies were soft, their heads and limbs were usually made of some sort of ceramic material and we had to be gentle. Our other baby doll, who suffered greatly at our attentions, was Brownie our dog. We'd dress him up in baby clothes and haul him around in a wagon. Poor guy, I know he hated it, but he let us do it until he just couldn't stand any more!

Then we all had one "girl doll", about sixteen inches high, for which dear Mother made little clothes from whatever scraps happened to be lying around. We could even comb their hair - carefully! And we each had a little crib for our dolls. I moved mine with me for years and suddenly they were gone; to this day I have no idea what happened to this happy part of my childhood.

Our favorite indoor pastime was and still is reading. In the winter, I easily read a book a day. Our folks usually gave each of us a book every Christmas, and we treasured them for years. I hated to stop when it was time to do chores! I whizzed right through whole series of books like "Dottie Dimples," "The Campfire Girls", "The Bobbsey Twins", "Nancy Drew", and the Gene Stratten Porter series about "The Girl of the Limberlost". I've kept on reading ever since; when my boys were little I read a lot to them, and they were all good readers.

Other indoor games included "Playing School" and "Playing Store". Playing School didn't last too long - maybe a half hour at most - because whoever was the Teacher that day always got too bossy and we Students simply staged a revolution. Playing Store though, was fun - and probably very educational too. We took great pains to find just the right sized boards to make shelves, and then we spent some time collecting some tin cans. We didn't have many because Mother and Dad canned so much of our garden each year; so cans were scarce in our house. Then we'd sit down and make our own money out of cardboard. We made "coins" of all sizes and wrote the amounts they were worth on each piece. We didn't make paper money; we thought it wouldn't last long - an interesting observation in the light of our government's fiscal policies today! And too, we rarely even saw money beyond what few coins Mother collected for our bits of chewing gum and ice cream cones when we went to town on Saturdays. So when the board game "Monopoly" came out, we were in heaven. All those bills!!! We felt rich just handling them, which may be why we played it often, sometimes continuously for days; it was our favorite indoor game. Close behind in popularity was checkers and a game called "Sorry".

And then, card games. Maybe it was just my family, maybe it was because we lived in such a cold climate and had to stay indoors a lot, but it seemed like every adult I knew (and I was related to most of them!) played cards. Whenever we got together with friends or family, the adults played cards, and so did the kids when they got old enough to understand. As kids we played Old Maid, and Spoons. Later we grew up and played Whist, Pinochle, Sheep's Head, Hearts, Seven Up, Oh Heck, and Bridge. And to this day, when I go to see my relatives in North Dakota, they still play cards, no matter what the occasion! It is as automatic as making coffee...and eating buns and bars!

When we were old enough we had piano lessons. Bob was exceptionally talented and took lessons seriously until he went to college, where he graduated with a music degree. I only lasted to Book Three of the John Thompson series. My teacher never said much, and I was bored, though I must say he didn't do anything to motivate me. Later I took clarinet lessons in high school but I never really got it right. I had a cheap instrument and was always breaking reeds; and besides I felt like I about blew my head off! So that too, slipped away from me. When I had choral music at my high school in New Ulm, Minnesota, I was hooked. I loved and still do love music with a passion. During my childhood years my folks tuned into the local music station, so I learned a lot from osmosis. I don't play anything, but I'm a fairly knowledgeable and a music devotee. Don and I have for years been season ticket holders (with our friends the Duesenbergs) to our St. Louis Symphony, ranked as one of the best in the world. We all love to go together to concerts.

Of course we had a radio - nearly everyone did, even in areas with no electricity. We had a battery operated unit even when we lived in Kensal and had access to electricity. It was a huge monster of an apparatus (the radio on one shelf, the cumbersome battery on a lower shelf, but we got fairly good reception. It was our lifeline to the world beyond our prairies. We'd pull up a chair or sit on the floor, with our ears as close as we could get them so we wouldn't miss a word. By the time we lived in Kensal, we'd begun to listen regularly to such programs as "Jack Armstrong", "The Green Hornet", "The Shadow", and the "Lux Radio Theater". When we were younger, we didn't listen much; we weren't interested and didn't have time for it. How could a radio soap opera compete with a water fight?!

Movies were a rare treat; we didn't go to see them very often, maybe once or twice a year when my folks felt a film was worth our driving all the way to our town or a distant one. Real theaters as we know them today were rare. Usually there was a building designated as the "show hall". By the time I saw movies, we had sound, but my parents remember the silent movies, during which someone played appropriate music on the piano; it was romantic during the love scenes, scary during ghost scenes...and you had to read the lines they silently "said" in captions at the bottom of the screen. A far cry from vast multi- screened cinemas we have today! I do remember seeing a few Walt Disney films like "Pinocchio", "Snow White", and "Cinderella", some Shirley Temple movies, and later "Little Women", which just broke my heart when Beth died. I cried for hours afterward, and choked up inside for days whenever I thought about her.

Outside, the world was ours - or at least five kids on top of a box car in North Dakota thought so. Tomboy that I was, I loved to be active outside and was never happier than when I was running wild and free through a field or swimming in a pond; some days I just had to move!

When we lived in Deep we had to walk across a half mile of field and then a mile of Soo Line railroad tracks to get to school. One of our entertainments was to see how long we could walk on the rails before we fell - or were pushed off by a rival sibling. Most of the time the Soo Railway Company had a box car or two sitting empty on these tracks, and naturally we assumed they were for us to climb on - which we did with great excitement. ("We" consisted of the five Leiningers and three Miller kids and the Wagner girl who used to walk part of the way home with us.) We'd get on the top and thrill to see the prairies from this high up; and then we'd walk along its narrow plank for a little extra drama. None of us ever fell off, but I suppose that would have been little comfort to our mothers who would most certainly have told us it was dangerous, had they known about it.

We had several organized games we liked to play, one of which was "Ante-I-Over." We'd play on two opposite sides of the garage and throw a softball over the roof, and if the other side caught it they would run around to the other side and try to touch the player with the ball - then they'd be on our side. "I'll Draw the Frying Pan" sounds weird but we loved to play it; someone would pretend to draw a circle on your back and then punch you in the back, and you had to guess who punched you. If you guessed right, then that person was "it" and we'd all run and hide. If he found you, he'd run back to home base and say so-and-so was out. Another favorite was Kick the Can, which was played along the same lines except the persons not "it" would kick the can when the "it" person was looking for us, to put us "out." Finally "it" would find all the players and touch the can to put them "out." Needless to say, this was fun for everyone but "it!"

Now that I think about it, I realize that Bob and I really did spend a lot of time together, maybe because we were so close in age, maybe because I wished and half thought I <u>was</u> a boy, and I liked to play boy games. But it wasn't all one sided between us; he'd do some girl things with me such as playing paper dolls, and I did boy things with him. We played marbles a lot; in fact we seemed to be an even match in a lot of things. For example we liked to wrestle together - and I held my own, too! We sailed a lot of "boats" together on the rain filled ditches on either side of our graded gravel road. We skipped rocks too, when we found a slough, a feat I was not too good at but he was.

A word more here, about Bob, whom I love very much. Bob and father never got along very well. Dad had such big plans for the son and heir; too many plans, I think. Now I can see that Dad was trying to live his life over through his only son, which may explain why he had to be in control. And the more he tried to control, the more stubborn Bob got, and their fracases were not few. I can remember "arguing" matches between them, and Bob would lie on the ground and kick and yell as hard as he could. He wanted to be in control too. As the only male child of a family in a place where male children were revered, Bob had a difficult time. He got the extra responsibility to be everything his parents wanted him to be. I can remember Mother saying Bob this, and Bob that…it was clear to all of us girls that he was to be the one who would "amount to something." So as the male he was revered - and at the same time, ruled - deservedly or not. I'm not sure what Dad wanted of Bob - but he <u>was</u> going to get the education we girls wouldn't get; he was going to become some sort of professional, a pastor probably. Ironically, Bob did become a professional - earned a Master's Degree in musicology and now teaches music at his and Dad's alma mater in St. Paul.

Now, back to playtime! I took great pride in the fact that I was better than anybody else on the chinning bar; at least I thought so. Dad supplied the metal pipe and we set it up between two trees behind the chicken house. I remember spending hours practicing our antics on that bar during our summers in Deep. I could even hang from my toes with great agility - and tenacity. But there were many times when we got careless and fell off - once Lois banged her chin on it badly and scared us all - but it never seemed to affect our hard heads much!

I think basketball is probably <u>the</u> sport of most rural areas, perhaps because it is played indoors, despite any foul weather. When I was old enough, I played on the school's girls' basketball team in Kensal for several years. Girls played half court and I played forward. Dorothy and Lois were guards. One year I made the all star team for our district. We practiced several afternoons a week, so our study time wasn't interrupted. Then, on Friday nights we'd play a game with some opposing team from another high school, but always before the boys' game, which I guess people took more "seriously." Nowadays North Dakota girls play from August to November, and boys from November to March. Games were always well attended, and the cheering was vigorous. Most people had large families, and so a single player could have aunts and uncles and cousins and grandparents rooting for him or her, so there was lots of excitement and motivation. Going to the games is a family affair; to this day Ken and Hazel still go to three or four games a week to watch their various grandchildren perform. And they're seventy-five years old!! But basketball and cards, of course - can pass a lot of cold winter hours; that has never changed.

We were really in heaven when we went to visit our cousins in the Binford area because then there were so many kids that we could organize practically two softball teams if we wanted, which we sometimes did. But with so many young excited minds at work, we usually ended up breaking into various groups of mischief makers. I especially loved to play in the hay mow, the second story of a barn where farmers stored their hay for winter. And I liked the tree swing, made from a rope and an old rubber tire; so exhilarating to swing way up so high!! And as I've mentioned, we rode the calves, or later the horses, and played "Kick the Can" or went swimming in the slough, or - well, there was just no telling what we might think up. And often did, much to the consternation of our parents. (i.e. the green crabapple episode.)

We also had great times with the Brauer Boys, the name by which we in our family still call them today. There were five of them and four of us Leininger girls; now wouldn't that just excite any bunch of sisters to the core? They were pretty good looking too, and loads of fun to play with. Of course they didn't hesitate to let us know they didn't want to play with us; we weren't boys, for one thing, and we couldn't swim for another. (The Brauers lived within walking distance of the municipal pool in Minot.) At that time, I was afraid of water, but I wanted to learn because they were so good and could even dive off a high ladder at the deep end of the pool. I was so amazed! When I was about nine years old, I nearly drowned myself trying to "fit in" with the guys by swimming into the deep end, knowing I wasn't that strong of a swimmer. Somebody rescued me, probably one of the older boys. Embarrassing!

When we got a little older, we got to go to camp at Red Willow Lake some fifty miles north of Kensal. The camp was sponsored by the Walther League, the Lutheran organization for young people. The league was named after the first American president of the Lutheran church. The camps lasted a week, and the price of $10 included cabin sleeping, meals and all our bible study time and play time planned for us. We especially loved sitting around the campfire near the lake for our devotions, which included singing, a little special talk, and prayers. I loved camp. We played lots of competitive games with the boys, which I liked because by this time I was beginning to realize that boys had a new attraction for me. The hormones must have been zinging around because I sure kept a sharp eye out for cute guys -though there weren't very many! And I learned to swim, though I never got very good; I could only swim out as far as the raft, about fifty yards from shore. We did lots of water fights and water "drops" on unsuspecting pedestrians beneath second story windows. One summer I learned to roller skate and got very good at it; even learned to skate backward like the boys! I loved skating, and was able to perfect my skills and technique later at Spiritwood Lake, our favorite place to skate, which was a dozen miles south of our house in Kensal. Some weekends Dad would drive us over, and wait patiently while we skated, until the music stopped.

We did the usual prank things kids do at camp - like short sheeting the cots, sewing up pajama legs, teasing the younger kids in the outhouse. In cooler weather we'd have hay rides in the moonlight - so romantic; we could imagine we had a cute guy to cozy up to, but there just weren't very many! These hay rides usually ended in a straw fight - hardly romantic.

The Brauer boys, being in the same church circuit (by this time they'd moved to Monango, fifty miles away), always went to Walther League camp when we did, and we did a lot of things together. Don wasn't so good on skates, so I skated a lot with Fritz, his older brother. Only years later did I learn from my new husband Don that he was very unhappy about Fritz gaining all my attention, in fact, downright jealous. After all, I was Don's friend, wasn't I? He'd always thought so, anyway. The truth of the matter is, older girls like older boys, and my friendship with Don dwindled as I continued to gravitate to older boys; they could do more, they seemed to have such self-confidence, which I really admired. Just being with them, skating, teasing, running races, playing ball, made me feel confident and powerful too. I still was very shy about presenting myself "properly" to any young man, though I did have skate dates with a couple of the Brauer boys, even though they were much older,. Anyway, we knew them and they were "safe" dates; not too exciting. My sister Tudy, though, remembers being shocked and thrilled when she saw me kissing one of the older Brauer boys! (When? I've often wondered.)

To get back to skating. When we lived in Kensal, late on Sunday afternoons Dad consented to drive us over to Spiritwood so we could skate. We learned how to skate different patterns and figures, and with careful practice, we could follow the announcer's instructions as he called out each different one. Since there were usually a lot of people skating around us, we soon learned you <u>have</u> to be good just to keep up. We fell down over and over, but just kept getting up and trying again - until we were quite good. Good enough to let the eyes stray as we circled around and around - always looking out for nice looking boys. In those days, most girls had no standards by which to measure a "nice boy." If he looked nice, most of us decided to skate with him if he asked, of course. Lots of girls I knew just went right up to the boys and asked them to skate, but my sisters and I couldn't - even though we wanted to. We were too scared they would turn us down.

I've purposely saved the more questionable of our high jinx for last, maybe because some place deep inside me I still think we're going to get caught. For example, we had a party line telephone, which meant we shared the use of our phone with several other people. So when the phone rang, the call might be for the Gessners down the road, or the old man at the service station, in Russell, or someone else. Of course you weren't to pick up the phone if it wasn't your ring; so, for example, if the phone rang two shorts and one long, we knew it wasn't for us, and we were supposed to ignore it. Well - we kids didn't. Oh we were told not to, threatened with <u>punishment</u> if we did - but we did anyway! And oh the things we heard! All worth the threat of discovery, I assure you.

I'm afraid I now consider what we did to gophers an unkind prank against all gopherdom, though we thought it terribly fun and funny at the time, me especially since I prided myself as being every bit as clever and quick of hand as any boy. Such a tomboy was I that I challenged any female to drown a gopher as well as I could. When the ditches beside the railroad tracks filled with spring thaw water, we'd fill our lunch pails with water and flush their little burrow holes. Pretty soon a gopher, soaked and pretty upset about it, crawled out and looked around to see who was there. He saw us - and took off, with us gopher chasers in hot pursuit - usually Dorothy, Bob, and me. Dorothy was pretty game for most things; only sissies like Lois and Tudy hung behind sitting on the fence. Of course we chased it, but never did catch one; I suspect deep down we didn't really want to, and I don't think we ever did actually drown one. But the glory of the hunt! The thrill of the chase! That's what we wanted - and we got it. Gophers were so plentiful that I heard years later from Mrs. Hall, my friend Lori's mother, that at one time they offered 1 cent per tail, just to get rid of some! We did not know that (or Dad probably didn't tell us) or we might have become serious trappers in the fur trade for candy money!

94

Even though we liked school - liked learning, that is, - the school itself was hardly friendly to us. In fact, I don't think I ever remember it being <u>warm</u> in our school in Deep, which was small (just one room), but nonetheless cold. In Deep our teacher was also the janitor, and if he didn't get up early enough to stoke up the fire in the boiler, we knew we'd just <u>freeze</u> until noon, when it began to warm up a little. We all wore our coats and mittens until then; hardly conducive to learning or figuring with pencils and ink pens.

On any given day in our Deep school, just beyond the grain elevators and train depot, we might have as many as twenty kids. My "class" consisted of Theodore Miller, who lived near by, and me. Our teacher had to be pretty creative; it must have been exhausting work to teach twenty different kids at eight different grade levels, and all for a pittance in salary. I'm not sure our education there was awfully good, but we got what we needed to go into our school in Kensal.

All of us kids were good readers, probably because we saw our parents read a lot, or at least Dad did; and they gave us books as gifts at every occasion. We learned phonics early on, and really <u>loved</u> spelling, particularly spelling bees. We got 100% on most of our spelling papers, and we were usually at the head of the lines in spell-downs; the Leiningers were fierce spellers! We learned the multiplication tables well, probably because the teacher, and sometimes our parents too, would drill us over and over until we knew them all by heart.

Our teacher, Mr. Fursteneau, may have made us learn things, but it wasn't much fun for us, and I know it wasn't easy for him either. He would start classes one grade after another; I think we learned a lot just listening to the other kids recite things like the multiplication tables or historical facts. We Leiningers all excelled in technical things like math and phonics, but were not exactly stellar performers when it came to history or geography. I did manage to learn all the states and their capitals; but to this day I have trouble keeping my history sorted out. I wasn't into penmanship either…as any recipient of my letters will tell you. I think what made history so boring was that there was no discussion; the teacher just told us the facts and we were supposed to spit them back to him on demand. No questions asked; no answer but one. Not the best way to learn, but we did learn enough, I guess, to be reasonably good citizens.

Not everything I learned in school was beneficial, though…l Learned] early on that teasing can really cause pain. I remember one of the kids was a bedwetter, and his family wasn't very clean, either. So we'd taunt him with "Rickie stinks a lot like a pot!" until he just about cried. Once Tudy wet her

95

pants during reading class, and the kids began to tease. Later I loaned her my gym shorts which were about six sizes too large, but I knew she would just die if the kids kept it up.

The one experience of those early school days that has stayed with me the longest, and has had the most lasting influence was with our teacher Mr. Fursteneau. He was half caucasian, and half American Indian; and the adults called him "that half-breed" behind his back. I don't think any of us kids did, because I think we knew he knew what people said, and it hurt him. He had a small son, too, which may have been why he left after two years. He didn't want his little boy exposed to that kind of prejudice. That was perhaps my first experience with what we now call racism, and I've taken that with me into my life in the large midwestern city where I now live in a happily integrated suburb.

We also received a little newspaper in the mail put out by the national church body called "The Child's Companion", wherein were listed all the names of children who wanted to correspond with another child of the same birth date. For some years I had two pen pals, Joan Newbauer from Chicago, Illinois, and Myra Bitter from Sheboygan Falls, Wisconsin. We wrote and exchanged photographs, and became quite familiar with one another, though we never did meet. They might as well have lived on the other side of the world! We gradually lost touch and interest as we grew into teenagers, but my sisters and I still value these far away friends, who added a special dimension to our growing up. Perhaps they gave more to me than I knew at the time in that I knew very early there was a big world out there beyond our prairies - and that I was going to go "out there" someday, when I was grown up.

Another school year highlight was "Play Day", a day many schools set aside for competition in a number of events, including music, declamation and spelling contests, as well as high jumping, racing, broad jumping, etc. I might add here that some schools also had "Flag Drills", a day designated for reciting poetry in front of everybody (I hated this!) and did skits and spelling bees, I liked better. Lois was very good at declamation, and I wasn't at all. I just never could get much "expression" into some essay I was supposed to recite. Such work! I was much better at high jumping and cartwheels. Since I was taller and had longer legs than my older sister Lois, I could compete with my eldest sister Dorothy -and I can't tell you what joy that gave me, to compete with her and be as good as she was. And would you believe? At age thirty-five I could still jump over a five foot pole with no problem!

Chapter Eight

"I Wanna Grow Up!"

We moved to Kensal, back in the eastern part of the state, when I was about twelve years old - I was in sixth grade. Kensal was the first actual "town" I lived in, so a few things took a little getting used to. For example, Kensal was predominantly Catholic, and so had a big church in the middle of the town. There was also a Methodist church, and then our little Lutheran church, which looked like all the others - white frame, steep roof, three gothic windows on each side, and the steeple. There were no minorities around, like American Indians or blacks. And Kensal had its own sheriff, an appurtenance awarded only larger towns.

Living in a town meant larger problems in certain respects. For example it was in Kensal that we first saw real poverty and hardship. The man who lived across the street from us (near the edge of town) was the town drunk; he was also husband and father with a wife and five children, who suffered greatly because of his addiction. We'd hear him come home late at night, dead drunk....and wondered how on earth they got along. In fact, a lot of people who lived very near us, in the same block, had rough times. Their houses shed peels of paint and fell into serious disrepair. Funny though....while everyone saw this evidence of poverty, no one said much about it. The neighbors, the community, looked the other way, perhaps because poverty was tacitly thought of as shameful. My folks did their bit though by buying our milk from a poor family down the street who had a cow. Then there was Mrs. Hoggarth, who lived across the street from us. She wore layers and layers of old, smelly clothing, all filthy. She had few teeth, and muttered to herself constantly. We children were terrified of her because we thought she was putting a curse on us, or whoever crossed her path. She came over every day, as did several neighbors, for drinking water from our well. (This was common then, as not everyone had a well.) And every evening she came over muttering and squinting at us, to ask for our potato peelings so she could feed her chickens. Mother always had something for the chickens, and I suspect for her also.

Most importantly, the first thing I think of when I think of Kensal, is flipping on a light switch, and the room lighting up. Kensal eventually brought us the incredible, delightful luxury of our first bathroom!!! Running water and an inside flushing toilet with shower and tub - well! You can imagine our joy. When we girls had been in Kensal long enough to develop some friendships, we invited our girlfriends over for a slumber party, and all our guests wanted to take showers just to try it out; several times! I got upset because I thought they'd use up all the hot water. (Later I learned that it would refill and reheat itself in the hot water tank in the basement.) Kensal also offered some nocturnal adventures we wouldn't have dared in Deep. For example we took to some late night walks around the

99

neighborhood in our robes and slippers. We must have climbed out a window, though I don't remember exactly. Anyway, one night we got locked out of the house while my parents were gone. Marion Parrish, the teacher who boarded with us for one year, had locked the doors and gone to bed. We had to wake her up by banging hard on the door to let us in; she never did tell Mother and Dad. But she did warn us that if we did it again, she'd have to tell the folks.

The move to Kensal marked a number of changes for the family, but for me it marked the advent of adolescence and sexuality, neither of which I was prepared for at all. By age 13 I felt I'd had a hard enough time being a girl, but I soon learned that there was more in store for me than met the 13 year old eye. I have always felt more boyish at heart than girlish, and the constant cultural tug to be feminine and all femininity means has been a struggle from childhood on. Sometimes I've thought, wouldn't it be easier if I was just big and ugly? Then the outside would match the strength inside of me, and I'd be happier; so would everyone else, for that matter, because no one could be embarrassed by a tom boy who really was a boy. Then I would no longer have to fit my big self into the small image of the feminine role; I wouldn't have to be the perfect little lady my religion and my small town world required of me.

I'm sure the fact that I was the daughter of a Lutheran pastor made things harder for me than most other girls, though one must remember that churches held great social power in any small town in America. Catholics were very strict about adherence to doctrine, but so were Lutherans, who'd split, in fact, from the Mother Church centuries before. It took two marriages and several decades of Lutheran experience for me to finally see that pastors, particularly in my dad's time, were more domineering than nearly any other male social figure in my world. Farmers may have been chauvinistic at heart, but they were usually out working in the fields. It was the farmer's wives who held the real power in the family because they kept things going, they enabled all the rest to happen. But the pastor had much more time to direct and control. Yes, they preached on Sunday (which required study time), and they tended to parish needs, but generally they were at home more and under foot - or rather, on top of it. While my mother had more help from Dad in daily chores, she paid a high price. Dad ruled. Period. Mother had little to say about anything as all matters of family policy were dictated by Dad, and certainly all disciplinary measures were his alone. Mother was what God and the Lutheran seminaries decreed - a helpmete and mother of his children. This was also the case for most of the Lutheran wives and mothers I knew in that time, and it hasn't changed much in my lifetime.

I don't recall ever seeing my parents being affectionate with each other either. I do remember Mother coming into our room to sleep sometimes. Later I realized that she was following the edict of the church, which was that sex was only for babies. She'd had five in slam bang order and she'd had enough. And since Dad was trained in the practice of celibacy in lieu of babies, they simply cut that part out of their lives at certain times.

Anyway, back to the joys of puberty. Tall and skinny, with gold wire rimmed glasses and spaces between my teeth (couldn't even spit worth a darn between them), I was hardly a prize. Of course, I didn't care much until I began to like boys for more than drowning gophers or jumping fences; this happened, I think, when I was in seventh or eighth grade. As my body changed, so did my mind about boys. I felt very torn between the real me who just wanted to have fun, and the model me, who had to tone down, dress up, tease less, and do something about my "looks." What a drag, I thought. It seemed like I couldn't please the boys, or girls, for that matter; anyway, I was never popular with either. I certainly wasn't pleased with myself. But I immersed myself into my great and dependable loves at the time, basketball, roller skating, and high jumping. If I couldn't be a date or a cheerleader, I would be an athlete.

Well, my first menstrual period arrived when I was fourteen - a little later than most girls, I was to learn; and I had no idea what was happening to me. In those days, women would have died rather than divulge the fact that they were having their period this week. Certainly my older sisters Dorothy and Lois kept their bleeding a deep dark secret because I was completely ignorant of their periods or my mother's. What did they do with all the refuse from it? I couldn't imagine where they hid it so the rest of the family wouldn't know. When it happened, I went to Mother who said, "Oh? Well. Go talk to Dorothy." (Cousin Phyllis likes to tell a similar story. One day when she was about ten, she told her mother, "Mom, you're really getting fat." Her mother replied, "Don't you know what's wrong with me?" "No." "Go talk to your sisters." ! ! !)

Dorothy filled me in with the mechanics of what to do with this stuff; boy, some business this was, I thought. I could see even then that this was going to cramp my style and I didn't like it at all. I was enlightened by my sisters, but still had no knowledge of what all this mess was for - except that it had something to do with "PG". I'd heard that word whispered around among women; it sounded grave and deathly - disgraceful at best. I liked it when church ladies came to our house for a luncheon or a quilting bee; I liked to listen in and I'd hear things like, "Well, she looks a little PG to me," and then there'd be a lot of clucking.

Every once in a while I heard that some local girl had left town for a time, "gone to visit her Aunt Violet in St. Paul" was the explanation that went around. She stayed conspicuously absent for several months, and then there she was again. And then there were some short notice weddings, I remember. "Helen and Willy are getting married next month? Well…guess it's nice they've fallen in love so quickly!" Eventually I figured out what PG was: "Parental Guidance Suggested" indeed!!

Even though we all grew up around farm animals, we were never allowed to see animals give birth. Sex was never discussed in our home, and neither was Kotex, so I entered the fray of adolescence, zinging hormones, dating and kissing ill equipped. Once a boy kissed me and I was terrified that I was PG. What could I do? I lived in terrible fear for months that I'd have a baby because I'd let that happen. I knew how badly the "loose" girls were treated, and literally ostracized from society. My cousin Phyllis became married and pregnant very young, and though she stayed with the father of the child, a mere boy himself (who later grew into an alcoholic) the marriage was very unhappy. Somehow she stayed with him to rear five children, but her marriage was miserable. When we talked recently she expressed bitterness at the way she'd been treated in her day. Phyllis related, "A girl who got pregnant out of wedlock back then was scorned openly. Oddly, the same women who scorned me when I had to get married, now joyously treat their granddaughters to a big church wedding with the white dress and all the trimmings - even though those girls are as pregnant as I was. So, some things change, even in little North Dakota towns. But what really got me back then was that the impregnators, the boys, never suffered a moment for their 'crimes' of passion; that has not changed - anywhere."

I remember one incident when I was on the basketball team. There was one girl we really needed because she was a good player. She was tall and big boned, kind of rangy - and as the weeks went on, she got heavier and heavier, especially through the tummy. (I began to watch mine closely.) No one said anything, and I just thought she was getting fatter; no big deal, she was heavy anyway. When we made it to the big tournament, she was really big, but we needed her, so she played with us. Then she went home - and had a baby! And still no one said a thing.

It was this incident that helped me figure out just how you got pregnant. Until then, there were many days I'd walk around terrified if my period was late. What if it had happened? Did it float in the air? Like polio? I became painfully shy in those years, more reclusive, filled with shame at even the thought that I might be pregnant. I couldn't bring myself to ask anyone….Eventually I asked

Mrs. Thompson down the street who was a nurse and she filled me in at last! Still, there was something about boys that was dangerous; all we girls felt that. They were so attractive, so desirable - but drawn to them as we were, there was an element of danger about them, and I was a little afraid. Meantime, I kept growing and changing, looking for, and yearning after BOYS!

In the five years I lived in Kensal, I had seven kids in my class at school, and my teacher's name was Miss Otto; I remember her because she was so pretty and some part of my tomboy self wanted to be like her, but knew I couldn't. Academically, I still did well in reading, math and spelling; physically I still excelled in anything involving running and jumping or roller skating. I was involved with the Four H program where I learned a few basic home skills like sewing and hand work - I think I made several pin cushions, one of which I still have today! Of course I was still interested in boys, as I've said, but for entirely different reasons than previously. My gopher drowning days were over, and my days of puppy loving from afar about to begin.

One of the boys in my class was a nice looking guy who almost never smiled; so he was "out". Another boy I kind of liked was a big teaser; he sat behind me and always chewed Russian peanuts and blew the shells all over my hair. Another one was dark haired and very attractive, but when he walked to school, he literally marched. We knew this because he lived nearby, and his family came to get water from our well. His dad had been in the service, so he must have learned that from him - he seemed to be very proud of it. His twin sister was a good friend to me, but so very sad and quiet. I had other good girl friends, but mostly what I remember about those years, on a social basis anyway, was how shy I was, and kind of lonely. Other girls I knew had boyfriends and went on dates (my sisters did); some even went "steady." But I never had a special male friend, and was definitely very afraid of boys; the thought of being alone with a boy chilled me to the bone. What if I got PG like the girl on my basketball team?

My Dad allowed Lois and Dorothy to date local boys, as long as they weren't Catholic. He counseled church members whose children were dating to forbid them to date Catholics. He was true to his training, which years ago regarded the Catholic church to be an inimitable shame against the name of Christ, the Pope the anti-Christ. He hated it that Catholics thought they could buy their way into heaven. Anyway, if my older sisters even became friendly with a Catholic boy, Dad would step in - fast. For example, we (and every other girl in town) liked the Kulla Brothers - six of them at varying ages. They were good looking, and good at sports; sort of every girl's dream date. But they were Catholic. Well of course Dad got on his war horse and openly exhorted his congregation and anyone else who'd listen that intermarrying between religions was wrong, especially if one partner was Catholic. He actually forbade two couples that I know of from marrying. You can imagine how popular he was with the young people of his flock, and the town in general. He was so firm about it, so angry and adamant, that everyone was turned off. There was a great deal of resentment, even in the congregation, and in the end it all filtered down to us. We were so embarrassed, and none of us except Bob finished at the Kensal High School. We were sent to Dr. Martin Luther College, Dorothy and Lois as seniors, and later I as a junior and senior. Bob went one year and then went to Concordia in St. Paul, since he was thinking about becoming a pastor at that time. He was very young and probably lonely and changed his mind about the ministry. So he came back to Kensal and graduated from Kensal High School.

Since then I've harbored no ill feeling toward Dad about his stand on this - he was simply doing what he'd been taught. In his view - and the one handed him by his seminary - this was God's will. There wasn't anything else he could do, and still be a man of integrity, a representative of the will of God? But I think he could have handled it with less wrath, more tact and understanding. His departure from Kensal left behind some troubled and even hurt souls; probably not what God intended.

Dancing was just as bad, in his judgment. The word was not even whispered in our house. We wanted so much to go to parties where dancing was common, and to dances - like the school prom, but he held firm. My sisters got around this. When they arranged dates, they'd go with their local date to a dance held in another town thirty miles away. That way no local church member would see them and tattle to Dad, they thought; but sometimes it did get back to Dad, and they would get scolded. They still hold resentment about that - but they had to accept that this was just another facet of being a "PK", a preacher's kid. These dances were hardly sophisticated - the music provided by local fiddlers or a small band like the Burlesons - square dancing and some tame "Lindy" hop being the norm. Dorothy and Lois got to go to a few with boys who knew to keep quiet about it so it wouldn't get back to Dad. Once Tudy would get invited to a "party" at the home of her friend Karen Burleson, whose parents had the dance band. And she danced with Karen several times - why not? she thought. This is so much fun, the music so nice... since there were no "decent" boys around (none we were really crazy about) that night, a number of the girls danced together - a common practice for most women and girls, when young men were scarce because of the war. We three older girls did beg Dad to let us go to the prom; finally he said we could go, as long as we didn't dance. So we went - and we danced! I felt very guilty, but not guilty enough to be sorry I'd done it; and I had such a lovely time....Eventually though, Dad found out. I think a lot of this had to do with the fact that we were preacher's kids and had to set an example, which we thought unfair, as we knew members who did let their kids dance. So who said anything's fair...?

I should probably pause here a moment and talk about Bob, the son and heir to so many of my parents' expectations. They put a lot of pressure on him - Bob the Man, Bob the Bearer of the Leininger name. Yes, Dad did hope Bob would follow in his footsteps and devote his life to God as a pastor.

It was Bob's budding talent in music that kind of bound us together as a family in a way I think we're only just beginning to appreciate. Realizing early on that Bob was gifted with the piano, Dad himself taught Bob for some years. I loved to hear him practice....and remember especially his rendition of Chopin's "Fantasy Impromptu", with which he won a talent contest in North Dakota. This has always been a favorite of mine. My present love of music was born long ago, while Bob practiced, and then nurtured when we all gathered around the piano Bob played as we sang hymns or other favorites, like "Don't Fence Me In", or "Bali Hai" from the musical" South Pacific." Dorothy could play some of the pop tunes of the day, and two of us could fumble through some easy duets too (even I could play a simple one)! My parents both had lovely singing voices, much better than any of us except Tudy, who is a regular in her church choir now. Dorothy sings in a select Women's Chorus (I used to sing in our choir until about eight years ago.) The nice thing about these little singing times was that my mother would join in. She always seemed so pressed with household and church cares, that she never let herself enjoy the moment, just let herself be <u>happy</u> for a few minutes. But when she came in and sang with us - I know we all felt a special closeness we rarely achieved in our daily routines. Now that Dad is gone (1985), we've only gotten together once as a family, and we haven't dared try to sing; the hurt is still there. But we will again, I know. Music heals.

I was about to turn ten years old when the Japanese bombed Pearl Harbor in Hawaii on December 7, 1941. Much of the war went right past me until near its end, when I was about fourteen. It didn't seem to touch our community though...we didn't know anybody personally who had to go into the service. My parents and other adults talked about the war of course, and I was sad because of all the killing going on; but the politics of it all, and the details of its progress escaped my young mind.

105

We didn't have TV, and my parents didn't take a newspaper, so we got most of our news from the battery operated radio. I can remember sitting around it on the floor, my folks maybe in chairs, straining to hear and get involved in whatever was on, whether news or something like "The Jack Benny Show." Other than that, we saw only occasional newsreels when we happened to go to a town for a movie; newsreels were always run before the main feature.

Rationing became a way of life, so we didn't think much about it. The government handed out ration cards with letters on them. Dad was given an extra allotment of gasoline because he had to travel to visit members and preach, but otherwise we felt the pinch in items like flour, butter, and sugar. Mom had us girls stand in line for her to get rationed silk stockings. I don't know why silk was rationed, except perhaps for the reason that Japan controlled most of the southeast Asian countries where silk was made. (Nylon was then a new material which was not readily available to-the civilian public; it was used for parachutes in the war.) Waiting was a bore, but we did manage to get a few extra pairs for her - as a preacher's wife she had to look the part. These silk stockings ran so easily! If you can believe it, we could actually take the damaged stockings to a shop in town where they would sew up the run so well you could hardly see it! (And we toss our nylon panty hose out if they snag!!) Years later, when I was in nurses' training, I heard about the "Silk Stocking" churches (Lutheran) in St. Louis, (the rich belonged) probably named because during the war, their lady members were rich enough to get all the silk stockings they wanted - even in wartime! The war also shifted the local manpower supply, in that a lot of vagrant men (called "hobos") left over from the Depression, finally found work either in the service, or as regular farm hands, not just migrant harvest help. I remember something too, that has stuck with me for years, just as the demeaning remarks people made about our "halfbreed" schoolteacher. Of these men, who, when they could, worked on one of Roosevelt's CCC projects until it ended and then were left to drift again, people said "Oh, he's just a good for nothing bum", or "Oh, he'll never amount to anything." A mother of three sons myself, I know how terribly damaging and hurtful that sort of attitude can be and it is the attitude, the body language, the tone of voice, that kills something in a boy, a man. I've been mindful of that ever since. Oddly, no one ever said anything like that about girls and women. I guess it was taken for granted that females were already good for nothing anyway!

As I approached my junior year, Lois her senior year and Bob his freshman year, it was decided by Dad that we would all go to Dr. Martin Luther College (D.M.L.C.) in New Ulm, Minnesota. He had sent Dorothy there the year before, and she'd been so positive about her experiences there in some wonderful letters

106

and snapshots of her being a cheerleader, that he felt it right to send us also. No Catholics around, at any rate!

I don't recall any particular eagerness to go away from home; in fact, I was a little scared. Dorothy led the way, but I wasn't pretty like she was, and I didn't have her nice, thick, beautiful long brown hair. And I did have that big space between my front teeth, about which I was very self-conscious. I was just fifteen when my folks packed Lois, Bob, and me up and drove us to my first experience with dorm life a life that was to span over the next seven years.

The campus was beautiful, set on a hill top above New Ulm, Minnesota, and affiliated with the Lutheran Church – Wisconsin Synod. It was even more conservative than Dad's seminary in the Missouri Synod. The college president, Dr. Schweppe, must have thought us to be a great phenomenon. Here he had all these North Dakota Leininger kids whose preacher/father, trained to be less conservative, couldn't find a school strict enough for his brood! What were they, some wild tribe from the sticks who needed straightening out? Well, if he thought so, he didn't act so, because the teachers at DMLC, all men, addressed all the students as Mr. or Miss. It was so strange to be called "Miss Leininger" that often I didn't answer because I, Rose Marie, hadn't been called upon! It took me a while to learn my new name. One of the first things we found out was that a "C" in religion was the best anyone of the Missouri Synod persuasion could hope for.

I do give DMLC much credit for teaching me things I've come to appreciate over the years. (Though we kiddingly referred to it as "Dead Man's Last Chance.") I learned Latin and German, and had my first major exposure to good music and the fine arts. I was in the Aeolian Choir, which was all female. We generally appeared together with the men's chorus, called Marluts. We sang in formals on many occasions, often to the accompaniment of a huge pipe organ built into the stage of the chapel which also served as an auditorium. I loved to hear students play this huge creature it was so thrilling, shook you right down to your core. And I loved to hear them practice too, in the practice rooms which were kept locked, to be used only by music students. I thought, if only I could play the organ like that, even just the foot pedals..I'd feel powerful! I especially remember Wayne Schmidt, a graduate student who, though a small young man, could play that big instrument with the olympian energy of someone twice his size. Ironically, he now lives in St. Louis where he plays the organ and directs the choir at Concordia Seminary!

My music teacher, Professor Backer, also taught us how to recognize each instrument of the orchestra and where it was located. Later we were quizzed on this, and I always did well. It kind of grabs at my heart to realize that if I'd stayed in North Dakota all my life, I might never have been exposed to fine music - and the great joy it brings to me might never have become a part of my life. I shall always thank my parents for making it possible for me to go away to school those two years, because they probably changed the course of my life. How could I live without music?!

I did miss my home and family, but then I had my sister Lois, and for one year, Bob, close by, and we made sure we bumped into each other during the day. I most definitely did <u>not</u> like dormitory life, and I did not like eating in a big dining hall with a big bunch of other students. Most of the kids complained about the food but I never minded it. To save on money, though, the school placed bowls of molasses on half the tables, and bowls of peanut butter on the other half. Most of us hated molasses on our bread, and we'd end up passing the peanut butter bowls from table to table, and sometimes we fought for them (very quietly, I assure you.) Of course a lot of other food was served, but we Leiningers liked our bread. (No ketchup bread snacks here, alas.)

I wrote a lot of letters, and sent my laundry home in a big canvas duffle bag every week. My dear parents washed three canvas duffle boxes of dirty clothes a week, and then ironed them, re-packed them neatly, and sent them back to us, always with a home made treat, cookies or fruit. Lois and I usually shared our treats with our dorm mates.

Perhaps one of the best things to come from our years at DMLC was the correspondence between us kids and Mom and Dad. They wrote us often, and I for the first time shared some of their inner feelings on a number of things they'd never talked about much when we were home. We kids did too, I think, me especially. I learned not to take anything for granted - there were no telephone calls home except on rare occasions for some emergency. The only telephone was down in the dorm matron's office. She listened in on each conversation, so there was no privacy even if you did get a call.

The daily routine was pretty strict - and hard to take, at first, for this country girl who was used to running out the back door and across the wide prairie, when she was so inclined. Everybody was up at seven a.m., and down to the general bathroom shortly thereafter, where we shared four sinks, four toilets, and several showers. My sisters and I posed no problem to the rest of the girls, as we were not used to much extra washing at home. We washed our hair once a week, and had a weekly shower - after we got used to having all that water just <u>there</u> for us. (We'd only had electricity in Kensal for three years, and still had no running water or indoor toilet when we left.) As you can imagine, it didn't take long for us to get used to these luxuries!

Nothing could really relieve the very real loneliness and homesickness of being away for such long periods from Mom and Dad. A country girl, I felt very uncomfortable with the city girls, and my first roommate just about drove me away. It was her first time away from home too, but she was from some city, and very "worldly." All she seemed to do was practice her make-up techniques in the mirror, though makeup was greatly frowned upon by the school. Later I got a really nice roommate, Myra, and she was from the country too. I often went out with her on weekends to her family's place; we had some very special times there. I went to visit other friends' homes too, occasionally, and this helped me feel more at home, and less homesick. We did take the Greyhound bus home for Thanksgiving and Christmas, though, and were ecstatic by the time we got there. Home! There's just no place like it when you've been away for a long time.

Back to dorm life. We had classes all day, and study hall from seven to nine p.m. every evening. Study hall was just one large room where we <u>all</u> did homework in complete silence. Then we had one hour to get ready for bed, and by ten, our dorm matron Miss Ingebritson, "Inky" to us, came down the hall to enforce the rule of darkness. All the light switches were outside our rooms in the hall, so precisely at ten, she came down the hall and turned each light off one by one. I never recall a single "good night" or a kind word. It was strictly business - someone had to do it - and she proudly accepted the call. Unknown to her, I'm sure, were the many nights some of us sat up under the covers with a flashlight, studying for an exam the next day. And if we were caught out of our rooms, or had otherwise committed some infraction of the rules, she "dormed" us - which meant we had to stay in all weekend and study.

By the end of my senior year, the girls in my class felt we knew enough about Inky and had enough courage to fool her. So one spring night we climbed out one of the dorm windows and stole away to the park where we had a picnic - in pitch dark! Well, we knew others had done it, and since the park wasn't far we thought we could pull it off easily. And we did - except we were scared to death some <u>man</u> might get us! Later we found out there'd been a Peeping Tom cruising around the city in a certain car, and we girls were warned to be careful. Ha - if they only knew!

My social life at DMLC was a little spicier than in Kensal; I did have a few dates during my time there. I didn't like to go with a boy more than four dates, though, because they always wanted to do more "necking" than I cared to do. There were a couple of guys I really liked, and wanted to be friends with, but I was just too shy and terribly conscious of my front teeth - could hardly converse and certainly kept smiles and laughter to a bare minimum, or if I did, I'd cover my mouth. My folks just couldn't afford to have my teeth fixed; in fact they could hardly afford to keep the three or four of us at DMLC.

We rarely had any spending money. I might write home and ask for a little change to buy toothpaste with, or something else essential. All our other needs were taken care of, so I rarely went to a movie or bought a treat in town. If I wanted something very much and Mom and Dad agreed, they'd scrape up the money somehow so I could buy a new dress or new shoes. I remember getting very excited over each of these personal purchases, and I cherished them for years. I never even <u>thought</u> about putting on weight - because above all I knew I couldn't buy bigger clothes! Since I was active then and always have been, I've been able to keep my weight at 120 to 130 pounds all my adult life. Maybe it was the way we were trained to eat, or maybe just genetics, but none of us ever gained weight. I can remember Lois, who was shorter than I, exercising a lot at school so she could stay in her winter clothes. She used to sit on the floor and role on her hips to try and take any fat off her behind! I never had to work at staying trim, but she did and in her years at school she never became too heavy.

During my years in New Ulm, I did take a part time job on the weekends for a few weeks. I was a waitress in a cafe in the center of town, and it was a good long walk from campus, though I loved to walk. But it proved to be too time consuming, and since my studies were more important, I quit. We walked everyplace; I don't remember even getting in a car while we were there. Every cent counted, and I can remember digging around in the bottom of my purse for spare pennies so I could buy a three cent stamp to send a letter home.

June 10, 1949 - GRADUATION! I left DMLC without honors, but a good hefty string of As and Bs, with an occasional C. We had some brilliant boys in my class (one we called Einstein) - few of us girls felt we could compete; but I was happy with my record. Graduation was a thrilling three days of festivities, which included formal concerts with the choirs (I was an alto), the band and the organ all rendering their best of sacred and secular music for family and friends. My class numbered about sixty-two, and I will never forget parading into the ceremony to "Prelude and Fugue" played on the organ by Professor Albrecht. Just about everyone cried; I know I'd never had such a feeling of accomplishment.

Mom and Dad and some of the family came, and there were lots of snapshots taken. Bob came with a couple of his friends whom I'd met on a brief visit to him in St. Paul, which wasn't far away. (I'd stayed with Dad's brother Uncle Al, and his wife Aunt Irene.) It was the most wonderful day of my life, I think, up to that point; and I was ready to fly!

By the time I'd graduated, I was already strongly thinking about becoming either a nurse or an airline stewardess. A lot of girls aimed themselves in this direction (and also teaching) - these were the sorts of jobs you took until you got married, at which time you quit work and had babies. I didn't really think much beyond a career though; I wanted a profession of some sort, at least for a while. At that time, stewardesses had to be nurses, so in my work at DMLC I had taken care to plan my courses so that I would be ready for nursing school. For example I found my Latin classes were a tremendous help. But where would the money for school come from? I didn't know..but if other girls got the money together, so could I. For the answer to that mystery, you'll have to read on!

Chapter Nine

"Night and Day, You Are The One...
Only You Beneath the Moon and Under the Sun..."

After graduation from high school at Dr. Martin Luther College, I went home to plan my future. I knew I wanted to be a nurse, why I'm not sure. Maybe it was my fascination with the nuns at the hospital where we took Dorothy when she got so terribly sick; or the time or two we made other visits to hospitals close by. Anyway, I wanted to be a nurse and even though I knew I was well prepared to go into nursing school, I lacked one major pre-requisite: MONEY. Where would I get the tuition? I didn't know, but in the mean time I talked with Mrs. Laatz, the wife of the Lutheran pastor in Binford, who had graduated from nurses' training in St. Louis, Missouri. She encouraged me to set my sights high, to try for a good school even if that meant going far away. Well, to this country girl, St. Louis was the other side of the world.

I talked with her a lot, and with my parents even more - and at last I came up with a game plan. I loved games, as you'll remember, but this one would be for keeps in Life's big tournament. I decided to go to Jamestown College, which was just thirty miles from Kensal, for one semester, and then go into the practical nursing program at Miller Hospital in St. Paul, Minnesota, which started a new class every semester. My reasoning behind this? 1.) I could try out the one year of practical nursing, and if I liked it, I could go on into a diploma program later to become a Registered Nurse. In the mean time I could earn money working as an LPN. Money was always a problem, even though tuition at DMLC was inexpensive. Mother inherited a small amount from her father when he died, and this came in handy for all of us. 2.) I would find out this year if nursing was for me. I had no idea really, just that budding interest from childhood. Dorothy had done some nurse's aid work after her graduation and had liked it, so I thought, if she liked it, so would I. Then she turned to teaching as did Lois, so -well, there should be one nurse in the family, shouldn't there?

So - I was off that fall to Jamestown College, and some preparatory classes that would help me in my future life as a wife and mother - like "Etiquette"; wouldn't want to set a table incorrectly, now would I? What I really loved was choir. I joined the campus chorus and sang in a few concerts. I learned how to play ping pong, which I pursued with great vigor - 'cause I was good at it! To this day, even though I haven't played regularly in years, I still enjoy a good hard game of ping pong, and I feel good about that. In order to help keep a little pocket money around (my folks paid my tuition, which was quite low then, in 1949), 1 got a job as a waitress in the fancy restaurant in the Gladstone Hotel, which turned out to be the best eatery in town. It was also where the Greyhound buses stopped and let off their passengers for a rest stop. Sometimes they ate and left nice tips, but we waitresses got really excited when the local businessmen came in with their families - they always left nice tips, as much as <u>fifty cents</u>!

115

That was a lot in those days, and I put all my tips into my glass piggy bank which I'd had since childhood. It was a good way to save because you couldn't get the money out of it very easily. When I was about to leave for my full year LPN training, Dad helped me to ease it out through a slit in it's back. I found a tidy little sum in there, well over 100 dollars. And would you believe I saved that pig, hauled it around with me for many years, unable to part with it? In fact, I probably still have it!

During my four months at Jamestown I had a couple of dates, and did get to go to a college dance that Christmas. For a few hard earned dollars I was able to buy the most wonderful turquoise satin (with French ruffles) dress - which was just heaven to me. I saved it for a long time, and wore it to a number of parties and dances through the years; I think I finally gave it to Good Will. Another dress I loved was the filmy pink backless gown I wore to both Dorothy's and Lois's weddings. (Can you imaginewearing the same dress to both your sisters' weddings. This would be considered poor taste today, simply not done.)

I was beginning to learn about the world out there, or at least the one outside Kensal, North Dakota; and I liked it out there, loved the chance to learn. So when the time came to go to St. Paul and Miller Hospital, I was ready. As luck would have it, a cousin of mine, Betty Rahlf, also a country girl, wanted to get into practical nursing also, so we roomed together at the hospital. She had never been away from home before, and those first months were very hard for her. I was lonely too at times, but I was a veteran of two years of boarding school and could handle it better. I talked hard and fast to keep her there, and we had many crying sessions, but she did stick out the year. I was so glad - I didn't want to be alone either!

My memories of that year are all good; it was a year that opened my eyes to another world. I thought my instructors were nearly goddesses. All in white, they were, and so intelligent! (For women!) I was in love with them all, and studied hard to please them - I didn't want to let them down. I received good grades, and did well on floor duty; I was happy. I remember how odd it seemed to walk into a patient's room and introduce myself as "Miss Leininger", and then tell him I'd be doing his bath! Gosh...I can never articulate the anxiety we both felt at that moment. (Was I really cut out for this?) But my instructors gave us a lot of emotional support, and we all knew we were feeling the same thing. And if they could do it, so could I.

I've often wondered at my dogged pursuit of things, the sense of competition, the need for achievement the tom boy always had within the young woman. I knew I'd been given equal talents so there was no reason to have such low self-esteem - except for my teeth. They really held me back, I realized; it was so hard to get beyond them. So, as I'd always done in the past, I turned in another direction and said, "Well, how do I get this fixed?"

I asked one of the instructors, who recommended I see a Dr. Baker, an orthodontist on staff at the hospital. He gave me a good look, said he thought he could fix it up nicely, and popped me into braces, which I wore for a year. He charged me a minimal amount, I know, because Dad talked with him about how to finance the treatment. My parents didn't have any money to spare, but I was desperate, and they knew how much this would mean to me. In fact, it changed my life. I wore the braces, the rubber bands, the retainers, and at the end of the year, the space between my teeth was wide enough to replace that long lost tooth. Then Dr. Baker sent me to the Dental School at the University of Minnesota, where the clinic made the most beautiful bridge I ever saw, to fit right into the new space! The students were so proud, because hardly any of the gold showed at all, yet it made it strong. My shyness, my self-conscious tight lipped smile just vanished with the first look in the mirror; in fact, I kept looking in the mirror for days, just to make sure it was still there!

It took me a while to get over the embarrassment of those early years, but my self-esteem grew and grew, and to this day, when someone tries to make me feel bad about myself, I will not allow it to happen. Somehow, I have been blessed with the will and strength to go through all the trials of life, but that new smile marked a turning point for me. Armed with a new smile and my trusty talents, I knew I could get through anything.

I know that this eighteen year experience with my gap toothed mouth made me much more sensitive to the hurts and pain of others. I prided myself on the personal care I could give, though as nurses we were warned over and over not to get emotionally involved with our patients. I heard that, but couldn't feel it - it seemed so directly opposed to my sensitive, empathetic nature; how could you be a good nurse and not sob with your patients' pain? Yet I made myself pay attention to the warning. Later, in my three year diploma program, nurses who could not "harden up" were dismissed. Personally, I think an empathetic tear or two with a patient is entirely appropriate on occasion. But I have never let myself enjoy the luxury of it. The fear of dismissal is still very strong, and I would never dream of jeopardizing a job and work I love so much. Those who know me will attest to my ability to fall apart and cry easily on many family occasions; but not once have I ever shown a lack of emotional control in any medical setting. I am quite sure this manner is still taught today, in nursing schools everywhere. A nurse must be able to react quickly to any heartbreaking case or emergency situation. To do that, a nurse must be strong, and, alas, a little bit heartless.

I should probably pause here and talk a little about the politics of nursing and hospitals. Oh, I could fill volumes with tales of all the patients I've handled over the years, all the doctors I've worked with, but what I want to talk about is more important to us as a society, as human beings. I know that God gave me my talents, my skills and strength, in order to fulfill needs here in this life. I worked hard, studied long months and years (over four years, with refresher work when needed) in order to perfect my abilities. Yet we nurses are traditionally looked down upon by the physicians we work with. In those days, we were all supposed to jump up like jack rabbits whenever a doctor came into the nurses' station. And to this day, when a doctor walks in a room, my instinct is to stand up and await "command." I know I talked about this a lot when my boys were growing up, and now that my son Gregory is a doctor, I know he is especially sensitive to nurses. He's told me, "I am, because you've asked me to be!"

During my year of practical nursing I had no dates that I remember - I didn't have time! Still, we girls would gather in somebody's room and have a good gab session over patients and boys, or the lack thereof. A couple of the girls could tell jokes really well, so most of us would seek them out just to have a laugh and ease the tensions of the long day's routine. But we were learning so much, too much to have time to be even tired, some days.

That year of training at Miller was a happy one, and for graduation in January of 1951, my parents and my cousin's parents and other assorted relatives all came to the big city. It was such a happy time, and I felt so good about myself. I'd worked hard, and reached my goal - and had a bright new smile to boot! Then I worked for six months for the hospital as a practical nurse. I took the licensing exam, passed it, and became an official LPN; at last, my own cap and whites!

During that year at Miller, I began to think ahead toward further training. All my instructors had been R.N.s, and I admired them enormously. And too, I wanted to know the reasons why behind certain symptoms, certain theories, treatments, and surgeries. I wanted to know more about everything medical - the wheels of my mind were spinning.

Not so fast that I couldn't get excited about Dorothy's wedding, which was to be that June. She was so beautiful, and her Wally was tall, dark and handsome. They had met while he was doing his "field work" in North Dakota, where he traveled on his motor cycle!! Dorothy had been teaching in Mt. Clemens, Michigan, but was home for the summer in Kensal. They bumped into each other at a preachers' get-together. Gosh, what else could you want in a man? A good looking, prayin' man - with wheels! It was a good match, and both families were very happy. After their marriage they moved to Fargo, North Dakota, where Wally had his vicarage year before going to the seminary for his last year.

Well, as the wedding party assembled from far and near, I learned that one of the groomsmen was a good friend of Wally's and his name was Bill; and he was good looking and tons of fun to be with - and I just about dropped dead in my tracks at the sight of him. And, even more unbelievable, he liked me too! We teased and laughed and teased some more - both of us amazed at our mutual "find" - of each other. Even so, I held myself back. I was a very naive nineteen year old girl, and he was a twenty year old man, but maybe not so naive. The tomboy in me wanted to joke and have fun, but my sensible little lady self knew I should be careful. I couldn't have it getting around that Rose Marie was "fast." But there I was, my heart was beating so fast I couldn't stand it, and I knew I was going to give away my feelings about him - and then what?

After Dorothy's beautiful wedding at the church, we all went home for a lovely reception on the lawn. Afterward, Lois and I, Bill and another groomsman all jumped in Dad's car and, Bob driving, went over to Jamestown and Bill and I ended up on the campus grounds, under a moon as silvery as all the songs say it is. How could we ignore a scene like this? Well, the moon kept smiling down on us and we did some great kissing that night, and began what already felt like a thrilling friendship. I saw him several times that summer, and learned he was raised in a preacher's family (would I never get away from preachers?!) in Minnesota; so our backgrounds were similar. He taught me how to play tennis that summer, and he and Dad teamed up to teach me golf so I became good enough at each to play with him, and I was in heaven. How could I - tall, skinny, thin haired, gap-toothed me - have landed such a marvelous beau?!

Also during that summer, I finalized my plans to go into nurses' training in St. Louis. My parents, bless their hearts, agreed to pay the $100 tuition (total!) for all those years; can you imagine tuition that low? (I would have had to pay $500 if I'd chosen another program in St. Paul. The only reason I can think of for the low fee was that particular Lutheran Hospital was old, and wanted more students.) And Mrs. Laatz continued to encourage me; she had graduated from St. Louis' Lutheran Hospital School of Nursing just a few years before. I thought, if she could get through three years of schooling, so could I! I was so excited, and I knew no bounds. With my small savings, I was able also to buy a few new clothes and six student uniforms. Once I got to St. Louis, my parents would send a little money for essentials, and when I needed to, I borrowed from the Rotary Club. The rest was covered in the fee.

So off I went on a train from Jamestown, North Dakota, to St. Louis, Missouri - still a very young nineteen, with a trunk full of belongings and a whole lot more dreams. As the train pulled out of the Jamestown station, I could hardly believe this was going to happen - that I was actually going to achieve my goal and become an RN. Even though I did not know exactly how this was going to happen with so little money, I knew my parents were behind me, and I trusted God to take care of the rest. And He did.

Meanwhile, my friend Bill entered Medical School at the State University in Grand Forks. I think we both knew immediately that pursuing our goals was more important than pursuing our relationship. Even though we would have liked to see each other, there were just too many hard years ahead; we wrote and he telephoned, but we could not take the time away from our studies and responsibilities to meet. At one point he wanted me to meet him in Kansas City, where he had occasion to visit late in the year. But I could not take the time off, and I had no money for such luxuries. No man, I decided, was worth that long a trip. He pressed me to come, and I pressed to stay, so our relationship met its demise. I never saw him again, and I have wondered about him many times. I suspect that if we did meet, we'd have a very long talk punctuated with a lot of laughs, and besides he might even still be a bit handsome yet.

When I arrived in St. Louis, my Uncle Dick Torgler, as I called him, picked me up at Union Station, which, during and after the war, was one of the busiest train stations in the country. Whether going or coming to either side of the Mississippi, you almost had to go through Union Station. (When train travel ceased so dramatically with the advent of affordable air fares, the grand old building fell into disrepair. After twenty years, an east coast developer bought the place and made it over into a very exclusive, unique and beautiful shopping mall and hotel complex with dozens of clever shops and eateries, which attract visitors from all over the country. It's good to see that lovely German Gothic building come back to life, and reclaim a place in history. When I see it now, I remember how scared and already a little homesick I was that day!)

120

Uncle Dick was pastor at Emmaus Lutheran Church, but he was not of the mind that clerics should be solemn and stuffy. He could tell the greatest jokes - I laughed until I cried. His first wife had died; she was the sister of two aunts in North Dakota who had married Dad's farmer brothers. Now Uncle Dick was married to Aunt Etta (they wanted me to call them that, even though not related), who was quite a few years older than he, but was as lively and humorous as he. (Her first two husbands had died.) What a pair! Etta used to say that her favorite husband was her last. Anyway, they were literally my adopted parents during those early years in St. Louis. They did everything they could to support me, and Uncle Dick even contributed to my funding by paying me 50 cents a backrub! 1 also did some of their cleaning at times, or did her hair; whenever they needed some little job done, they asked me, knowing I did not want handouts, that I wanted to earn my way. We did a lot of things together - they took me to see local sights, had me over for dinner, etc. I learned quickly that they were well known in St. Louis. Their house was a big beautiful old place on Hawthorne Blvd., a private street in the Compton Heights area. It was owned by the church, and was tastefully furnished; no good Lutheran could ever be extravagant! But they were extravagant in their devotion to me.

As I already mentioned, Aunt Etta had outlived two husbands by the time she married Uncle Dick. I watched her, tried to emulate her, because to me, she was the ultimate example of what I thought was a "liberated", to use a sixties' phrase, woman. All the women I'd known in my childhood and youth had fit into two roles: they were either wives and mothers, a thankless job that wore them out into a premature old age; or they were spinsters, unmarried women who, if well off, took care of the family's cast off old relatives, or became a school teacher. I knew I didn't want either of those, but I couldn't see how I could be a professional nurse, a woman, and a devout Lutheran. Perhaps Uncle Dick was the reason, because he "let" her do anything she chose, so as attending shepherdess of Dick's congregational "flock" she knew no bounds. She was president of the Lutheran Hospital Auxiliary and was always involved in volunteer work. She also did work for the poor through what they called "City Missions". Her biggest financial success came through the making of "nurse dolls," adult girl dolls of molded plastic who could wear several costumes, for example, the student nurse uniform, the RN white uniform, and also a party dress. She and some other women made these in a sort of assembly line fashion in her basement. They sold these to the public; all proceeds went to the hospital, and they brought in thousands of dollars. She later turned the basement into a factory for the making of flower and bird "cages"; this time the basement was transformed into yet another "mill" of decorative delights. I still have a couple of dolls and cages, and will always keep them as a silent reminder of Etta, to whom I looked as a role model.

She knew every active Lutheran in the congregation, and made it her business to know the stragglers when occasion arose. Everyone adored her. You simply could not turn down a request of hers. I helped her when I could, but she didn't need my help. At that time she was sixty and going strong, but knew my need to feel useful. She outlived Dick, her third husband, and lived until she was ninety-five years old; while she was bed ridden in a nursing home, she still kept her sense of humor until the last. I have never forgotten her, and never will because she was everything I wanted to be - and am still trying!

My three years of training were difficult. I studied a lot and it was satisfying because I was finally learning the reasons why some diseases happened. Much of our initial work came as a review to me; after all I'd trained already to be a LPN in a large city hospital, so I knew about hospital life, how it worked, the whys and wherefores of basic nursing. Also I was a little older than most of my classmates, at nineteen going on twenty. Most of my class of thirty-nine girls was just out of high school and from St. Louis or surrounding rural towns. I considered some of the girls to be real snobs. They were either pastors' daughters, whose parents thought nursing school might sober them up a bit; or they were just into their cashmere sweaters, bobby sox and smoking. I never did smoke as I could not afford to, for one thing, and I thought it smelled bad. But most of the girls smoked - it was "in" then, and this was long before the Surgeon General's report connecting smoking to lung cancer.

Since there were more city girls than country, they tended to throw their weight around a little bit, and we country girls often felt snubbed, or put down. I know I must have seemed odd to them - two years older and already an LPN? Well, really! Maybe I could have handled my "seasoned" position better. Anyway, there were enough of this silent minority that we could band together for good talks if we needed. So we all managed to get through three rigorous years together without any major disagreements.

Dorm life and hospital routines were not new to me, but still the work and the hours were wearing. It meant studying late, rising early for duty at 7 a.m. to noon, and 4 to 7 p.m., handling all the meal trays, doing the morning baths, etc. Then came medications, shots, and treatment care. We did back rubs on every patient twice a day, even if the patient was up and walking, so that no patient would ever get bedsores; and too, the backrubs were relaxing. They got those rubs whether they liked them or not, because they were paying for them and we were learning to become good bedside nurses. Today, with nurses so scarce, these little things are done only if there is time, and only if enough staff is available.

122

We received experience in every field of nursing, from surgery to psychiatry. The operating room held considerable anxiety for me. I was afraid I would pass out, as I had done on a couple of other occasions, for instance, like my first time watching a woman in labor. I made it a point to talk with the nurse anesthetist, who was especially kind about my problem. She took me into the OR, briefed me on what would happen, and then she talked to me steadily during the whole procedure, and I got through it just fine. Mind over matter, perhaps; at any rate, I shall always be grateful to that nurse for helping me over a big hump of fear. As the three years progressed, we all found plenty of opportunities in sight and smell to get sick and pass out, especially when it was hot, but we didn't let that squelch us. I especially respected two of my nursing instructors, Miss Kubler and Miss Beckmann, who were never satisfied with anything less than perfection, and demanded excellence from all of their students. I still see them on a regular basis at the alumni meetings. In their evening years, they still remain active in professional nursing causes. These women are precious indviduals connecting my past to the present.

Our particular hospital was very old and not air conditioned. Part of our routine was to boil the glass syringes to sterilize them. If we were very busy we'd forget about them and they would boil dry - and all were lost. (We caught some heat about that, you can bet!) Otherwise, we also had to wrap the instruments, which had been sterilized in the OR autoclave, in sterilized towels. Hot work, in addition to our regular floor duties. We used fans on the floor but these gave only a little circulation to the heavy, humid air of a midwestern summer. What little air wafted in smelled of hops from the big Busch Brewery, which was not far away. It nauseated me. The summer heat in St. Louis (which no one had warned me about!) seemed intolerable to me - how do these people live through this? The 100 degree hot, dry winds of the North Dakota prairie were nothing compared to this. The humidity remained high summer and winter, I was to learn the first year. As the temperatures dropped, I kept thinking well, winter will be a snap after my winters at home. Wrong. I just couldn't figure out why I felt so frozen all the time when it was 30 degrees outside; but I learned. What I did love about the climate here was the early advent of spring - warm temperatures in March!! And now that I've lived here in St. Louis for many years, I can say the weather is OK, now that we understand each other...now that I have an air conditioned house, and an electric blanket.

I should mention too a couple of other aspects of nursing in the Dark Ages of the 1950s. One of the requirements for acceptance into the school was that you had to have your tonsils and adenoids removed. This was supposed to ensure that the student nurses would not always be getting colds and sore throats and thus be

123

out sick a lot, or spreading the germs to others. I had mine out with no problem, but other girls only traded one set of problems for another, and missed class anyway. Later, schools dropped this requirement - too many problems, too little theory. The other medical highlight of my training career was having my appendix removed, which was convenient since I worked right there. While the doctor rummaged around with my appendix, he also found some cysts on my ovaries, and removed them. I was a little concerned - I didn't want my fertility hampered, but I figured it wouldn't prevent me from getting PG when the time came.

So the time passed. I worked hard, studied intensively, looking neither to the right nor the left. Certainly I did share some laughs and funny experiences with my classmates, but for the most part, I stayed to myself; I just didn't have time for much socializing! I was not popular, but then I didn't need to be popular, as some of the girls needed to be - and I suspect they are still like that today. My top priority was to get good grades and function as a well trained, dependable and caring nurse - and this I accomplished. Our class still sends around a yearly letter written by one of the kinder and gentler of our group, who collects all our "news" and compiles it into a newsletter. She's been doing this for thirty-five years!

My social life was patchy, but I didn't mind. I'd date a seminary student occasionally and that was fine. Once I dated a seminary instructor named Fred and we seemed to hit it off well; we liked each other a lot. We went out a few times and then he ask me to quit nurses' training and marry him! No man was worth that, and I as much as told him so. Guess he figured I was like all the rest who were just going to work until Mr. White Knight came along and then marry and have little Lutheran babies. I said no and that was the end of Fred.

Toward the end of my training both sisters, Dorothy and Lois, ended up in St. Louis. Dorothy's Wally was here finishing his last year of training at Concordia Seminary, and Dorothy had just had their first child. Lois had just married yet another future pastor (it must be in the genetic coding of Leininger women), and had moved here also. Bill, a lovely man, finished his training too, while Lois taught school. Even though we were in the same city, we were all busy and really had to schedule our visits together. Bob was in the army, and Tudy was in college in Winfield, Kansas. The folks had just moved from Kensal to a country parish near Effingham, Illinois, called Island Grove, about 100 miles east of St. Louis. This was so nice for us, as we were at least within reach of most of the family. We were also close to Aunt Millie and Uncle Theodore Gutknecht. Uncle Theodore was the first Lutheran missionary to India. They were lovely people, a little older than Mother and Dad.

Then - I met Walt Oetting.

I saw him a few times reading, waiting in the nurses' lounge for a date. He was dating a couple of girls from the hospital and had dated one of the girls in my class. In fact, whenever I saw him, he was reading. He also wore this cap - a cap that I'd seen a lot of professors wear - it looked very academic. Irene introduced me to him as they were leaving for their date, and I must have taken mental note, even if unconsciously: always reading...that cap...hmmmmmmmm.

I did not see him again until that spring when I attended my brother-in-law Wally's seminary graduation. I was just finishing my second year of training, and Lois was preparing to marry Bill that June. Dorothy had had her first child, Paul, in January. Walt was just finishing his third year of seminary training and was to leave shortly for his vicarage year at Concordia College in Austin, Texas.

We bumped into each other on the campus, face to face. We had not seen each other since that fleeting introduction months before, but it was as if we had just run into a long lost friend. We joked, teased, and kidded around during the activities on the seminary grounds (which were and still are, exceptionally beautiful), but we both knew something was going to happen to us. By the time the festivities were over, he was referring to me as his fiancée. He was teasing, yes - but seriously teasing. I was carried away...this tall, dark, and handsome fellow with the most glorious wavy hair, with intelligence and wit to boot... Well! He already had a Master's Degree from Washington University in Ancient and Medieval History, so he was studying now to assure himself that, with further academic pursuit, he could become a professor of Historical Theology on any campus, in nearly any church situation. Like me, he'd pursued his goals, taking little time for anything else, until he was nearly within reach of full accomplishment.

Well, we laughed and just fell crazy in love that night, so much so that we couldn't find the way to Lois's future in-laws' place, where I was to stay. When we finally found their place, he carried me to the door; it was nearly five a.m. We were both so tired - and so in love - and then we parted. I did not see him again until mid-summer, but we wrote daily; each day's mail brought a letter more exciting than the one before. Then he wrote to have me come to Waterloo, Iowa, to meet his family, the Rev. Walter and Edna Oetting. I took the train (I decided this man was worth it!) and spent part of my vacation days, five I think, with him. Of course the anxiety of meeting his parents just overwhelmed me, but I decided it couldn't be as bad as the operating room. So what if the Reverend was the president of the Iowa East district of the Lutheran Church, and also head of the largest congregation in Iowa, and also charter member of the board of Allen Hospital, Waterloo, Iowa.

His mother was not there - she was helping her daughter Gloria with the birth of her first child, Paul. His brother Louis and sister Mary were there, and she and I did the cooking - neither of us very good. What a test for a future wife! I failed miserably, but I think it was at least edible. Walt and I were in love and not hungry, fortunately, though his dad looked me over some, I know. (Can't cook, eh? Well, what can she do?) But I could carry on a decent conversation, and Walt was obviously gone on me, so I guess all in all I was a fair catch for Walt who, he also knew, was not a man to be stopped.

He came to St. Louis to spend several days with me before his long and lonely trip to Austin where he would teach during his vicarage term of nine months. He was talking marriage right from the start, but now he was getting serious. He was the boss, and I certainly was willing. Next year, he said, before he completed his last year of studies at Concordia Seminary might be a good time to think about getting married. I would finish my training near the end of August. We said good bye; we wouldn't see each other until Christmas, four months later. We wrote every day; it did indeed look pretty serious!

Walt picked me up in his old '38 Ford at Christmas. This time I met his mother, the Lady of the Manse, the woman of courage and character who raised her four children and sewed just about every stitch on their backs. Some of this was necessary, but aside from that, she was incredibly gifted. My mother sewed entirely out of necessity; his mother sewed for the sheer joy of it. She'd rather be sewing, creating, than anything else, because at times I'm sure she felt the duties of a preacher's wife particularly demanding. Sewing either soothed or excited her - and the results were always the same: stunning creations, such as wedding dresses. (She sewed both her daughters' dresses and mine, with only a pattern and some suggestions, and a lot of faith that it would fit. I was never able to try it on until a few days before the ceremony and it fit like a dream!) She was easy to talk with, said she was "just common like an old shoe." Though she'd only finished sixth grade, she came from a well known St. Louis family, the Nolkempers, and worked a few years at the Brown Shoe Company in St. Louis before marrying the Reverend when she was twenty-two. She made a good pastor's wife, I thought - having her own "thing", her sewing, and yet able to be submissive enough to be unnoticed. Rev. Oetting was a powerful man and he never let you forget it. You wouldn't cross or challenge him and I didn't, though I wanted to a few years later!

It was during this visit that Walt took me completely by surprise and gave me a beautiful solitaire diamond engagement ring on Christmas Eve, 1953. He had planned it all; our love was sealed. I still couldn't believe it, even though that ring glowed on my finger. This naive country girl from a small North Dakota prairie town had come to the big city and had gotten her man; the man of her dreams, the man she deserved, for had she not studied and worked hard to achieve her goals? But nurse or not, she needed to become a complete woman, a wife, a mother. And she was ready for that.

We did not see each other again, except for a few days in June. I graduated from nurses' training in June, and completed the last requirement of floor duty three days before I got married. After we were married, he used to tell people that we saw each other forty days and forty nights - and then we were married - August 22, 1954.

Epilogue

"A little trick of laughing,
When all your cares go wrong,
A little smile of kindness,
Will turn into a song..."

This little saying was on a plaque which hung on the wall of our girlhood bedroom for many years. As I close this book of the first twenty-one years of my life, I now realize just how much that little saying has helped me through some very difficult years, as has my preacher's family, which has now separated to far distant points around the country. Like tumbleweeds in the wind, we learned very early to keep our roots shallow because life changes so constantly, and deep planted roots do not transplant easily. Little did I realize on my wedding day, that I would be called upon to make major adjustments so frequently as life unfolded. So as I prepare to move forward in my life, I am deeply grateful to my parents for teaching me an unfailing belief in values and a God who is always there, no matter how hard the winds of life blow...

MY GRANDPARENTS ON MOM'S SIDE
I knew faintly as a child.

I. EDWARD C. BEHRMANN
   Farmer in Indianapolis, Indiana
   Born: 1873, Indianapolis
   Died: 1943, Indianapolis (age 70)
   Married: May 3, 1990 to:

   EMMA REBECCA WAHLERS
   Born: 1879, Danbury, Ohio
   Died: 1937, Indianapolis (age 58)

Three children - all girls, in order of age:
STELLA   INEZ   HELEN (my mother)

   1. STELLA ADELINE
      Born: 1902
      Died: 1930 (age 28) during childbirth
      Married: to NORMAN EICKHOFF - second wife - OLIVE
                Businessman in Indianapolis
Two children - a girl and a boy

INEZ ALMA	NORMAN JR., EDWARD
Born: 1928	Born: 1930
Married: Bill Dougherty	Married: Marlene
Five children:	Three children:
Bill, Mark, Mary, Jane, John	Cathy, Eddie, Mike

   2. INEZ LOUISE
      Born 1904
      Died: 1922 (age 18), killed by a bus

   3. HELEN ROSE
      Born: June 15, 1906, in Indianapolis
      Married: October 26, 1927, in Indianapolis, to
      REV. WALTER E. LEININGER
      Five children:
         Dorothy, Lois, RoseMarie, Robert, Estelle
(See under Father's family for further information)
Mother (HELEN ROSE) now living in Yakima, Washington
(Mother's entire family was deceased by her age of 37)

MY GREAT GRANDFATHER: MICHAEL LEININGER
Born: Date ? in Alsace-Lorraine, France
Later farmed in Boone, Iowa
Buried in Boone, Iowa

MY GRANDPARENTS ON DAD'S SIDE
Died before I was born.

I. JOHN LEININGER
Farmer in Boone, Iowa, and Binford, North Dakota
Owned three sections of land
Born: 1858 in Boone, Iowa
Died: 1911 (age 53) Buried in Binford, N. Dak.
Married; 1880 to:

LOUISE STOLDE
Born: 1860 in Germany; later moved to Illinois
Died: 1927 (age 67) Buried in Binford, N. Dak.

Ten children - six sons and four daughters (all deceased)
MICHAEL, HENRY, JOHN, EMELIA, LOUISE, STILLBORN GIRL, ALBERT, WALTER AND
ANDREW (dad's twin), MARIE   (my dad)

1. MICHAEL D.
Farmer in North Dakota
Born: 1879 in Boone, Iowa
Died: 1952. Buried in Binford, N. Dak.
Married: CLARA GUTKNECHT
          Born: 1879
          Died: 1953

Eight children - two sons and six daughters
ESTHER, CARL, ALICE, CLARA, THELMA, ALFRED, GERTRUDE, EDITH

ESTHER married CLARENCE OLSON: Eleven children - Arthur, Irene, Robert,
Gloris, Donald, Carl, Esther, Richard, Avis, Linda, Melvin

CARL married HAZEL: Ten children - Imogene, Larry, Joyce, Kathryn,
Cynthia, Mary Jane, Roger, Nancy and twin girls (stillborn)

ALICE married BILL RAHLF: Twelve children - Kay, Dorothy, Ronald, Marilyn,
Patricia, Bill, Alice Marie, James, Jerry, David & Daniel (twins), Tim

CLARA married AUGUST RAHLF: Six children - Darlene, Betty, Theodore,
Paul, August, Clara Jo

THELMA married ADOLPH BERGLUND: Five children - Darrell, Lorraine,
Margaret Elaine, Ronald, Melody Ann

ALFRED married MARJORIE: Five children - Dennis, Michael Lois, Loren,
Peggy

GERTRUDE married WILBUR FADNESS: Four children - Michael, Richard,
Karyl, Steven

EDITH married Keith

2. HENRY C.
Farmer in Wheaton, Minnesota
Born: Date ? in Boone, Iowa
Died: 1934, buried in Wheaton, Minn.
Married: ANNA MILLER

Six children - three sons and three daughters
MATHILDA, PAUL, HERMAN (deceased), EMMA, EDNA, CARL

MATHILDA (TILLIE) married AUGUST VOGTS: Five children - Robert, Lois, Theodore, Betty, Kenneth

PAUL married EMMA REINKE: Four children - Ronald, Opal, Wilfred (deceased), Ervin (deceased)

EMMA married TED HOXTEL: One child - Dr. Eugene

EDNA married ARTHUR SLAGEL: two children - LaVonne, Donald

CARL married EVELYN GANGER: Four children - Daryl, Marlene, Fay, David

3. JOHN W.
Farmer in Binford, North Dakota
Born: 1883 in Boone, Iowa
Died: 1958, buried in Binford, N. Dak.
Married: IDA GUTKNECHT
Born: 1881
Died: 1975

Six children - four daughters and two sons
MARGARET, ALMA, TRES, ADA, KENNETH, REV. WALTER

MARGARET married ROBERT PARSONS: Five children - Shirley, Dolly May, Robert, Dianne, Joan

ALMA married BEN RAMSEY: Eight children - Gordon, Elaine, Phyllis, Rev. Jack, Rev. David, Mary Ann, Gary, Connie

KENNETH married HAZEL ROOD: Four children - John, Kay, Karen, Lynn

TRES married CLARENCE CHRISTIANSON: Two children - John, Sharon

ADA married JERRY MARTIN: Four children - Roland, Barbara, Rev. Daniel, Thomas

REV. WALTER married RUTH KNUTSON: Five children - Kathryn, Rebecca, Judy, Mark, Timothy

4. EMELIA (MILLIE)
Born: 1886 in Boone, Iowa
Died: ? buried in El Paso, Texas
Married: REV. THEODORE GUTKNECHT, Missionary in
India, 1908, pastor in Iowa and Illinois
Born: 1888
Died: 1960

Nine children - Five daughters and four sons
THEODORE (infant deceased), LOIS, MIRIAM, RICHARD, ROBERT, MILDRED, THEOLYN, LORNA, PAUL

135

LOIS married EARL SCHOENROCK: Two children - Joan (deceased) and James

MIRIAM married C. VERNON JOHNSON: One child - Cynthia

REV. RICHARD married VALERA: Four children - Sandra, Dr. Richard,
                                    Dr. Michael, Steven

ROBERT married LORRAINE CUMMINGS: Four children - Douglas, David, Candy,
                                    Melody

MILDRED married FLOYD DELL: Three children - Frederick, Dean, Cassie

THEOLYN married RICHARD SWEENEY: One child - Miriam

LORNA married MILTON EWELL: Two children - Rodger and Stephen

PAUL married BETTY GEARY: Five children - Christopher and Kimberly (twins),
                                    Kathleen, Karen and Kevin (triplets)

                    5. LOUISE
                       Born: 1888 in Boone, Iowa
                       Died: 1946, buried in Washington
                       Married: LEWIS SCHMIDT, Born 1877, Died 1933,
                                    Farmer in Binford, N. Dak; buried, Binford

            Two children - one son and one daughter
                       LEROY, DOROTHY

LEROY married MILDREN CLAUSEN: Four children - Myron, James, Lorna, Mary

DOROTHY married THOMAS MOORE: Two children - Bernadine, Roland

                    6. GIRL BABY (died at birth)

                    7. ALBERT A.
                       Born: 1890 in Boone, Iowa
                       Died: 1973, buried in St. Paul, Minnesota
                       Businessman in St. Paul, Minn.
                       Married: IRENE BEUTOW

            Four children - three daughters and one son
                       ELAINE, WARREN, LENORE, ALRENE

ELAINE married RALPH CLAUSEN: Four children - Nancy, Darryl, Cynthia, Nadine

WARREN married RUTH FRITZ: Four children - Nancy, Warren Jr., Donald & David (twins

LENORE married LESLIE HARTMANN: Eight children - Sherrie Lee, Janice, Craig,
                                    Lynne, Mark, Bradley, Steven, Lori
                                    Hans Greier (Godchild)

ARLENE married DALE CONNOLLY: Six children - Bruce, Brian, Brent, Beth Ann,
                                    Barbara, Barratt

8. REV. WALTER EDWIN (my father and mother)
Born: July 13, 1897 in Boone, Iowa
Died: January 25, 1985 in St. Louis, Missouri
Buried: Janaury 31, 1985 in Binford, N. Dak.
Pastor in Canada, North Dakota, Illinois and Minnesota
Married: HELEN ROSE BEHRMANN, October 26, 1927
Born: June 15, 1906
Died: October 26, 1993
Buried: November 3, 1993 in Benford, N. Dak.

Five children - Four daughters and one son
DOROTHY, LOIS, ROSE MARIE, ROBERT, ESTELLE

DOROTHY EMMA (sister)
Born: February 10, 1929, in Oxbow, Saskatchewan, Canada
Teacher and Medical Technologist
Married: June 17, 1951, Kensal, North Dakota, to REV. WALLACE MISTEREK
Pastor in Yakima, Washington
Born: November 17, 1926

Six children - Four sons and two daughters
Paul, David, Rachel, Tim, Deborah, Matthew

Paul married Maureen
Two children - Nathan, Cara

Tim - unmarried

David married Mari Huseth
Three children - Brian, Joel, Dana

Deborah married Rev. Daniel Adams
One child - Michaela

Rachel married Douglas Hovde
Two children - Alexander, Brandon

Matthew married Kari Graves
no children

LOIS LOUISE (sister)
Born: April 7, 1930, in Indianapolis, Indiana
Teacher
Married: June 14, 1953, in St. Louis, Missouri, to REV. WILLIAM KRENNING
Pastor in Camus, Washington
Born: February 20, 1930

Three children - Rebecca, David, Jonathan
Rebecca married Sam Sayers
David married Jennifer
Jonathan married Melissa
    One Child - Faith Hope

ROSE MARIE (author)
Born: December 12, 1931, in McNutt, Saskatchewan, Canada
Registered nurse
Married: August 22, 1954, in Island Grove, Ill., to PROF. WALTER WAYNE OETTING
Professor at Concordia
Seminary, St. Louis
Three sons
ROBERT, MARK, GREGORY
Born: April 25, 1929, in
Davenport, Iowa
Died: February 24, 1964,
in St. Louis
Buried: Feb. 28, 1964

MARK LOUIS OETTING
Electrician, Springfield, Missouri
Born: April 9, 1956, in South Bend,
Indiana
Married: April 12, 1986 , to
Sharon Sue Stafford
Born: May 18, 1954, Springfield, Mo.
No children

ROBERT WALTER OETTING
Born: December 13, 1954
South Bend, Indiana
Unmarried

137

DR. GREGORY MARTIN OETTING
Neurosurgeon in Richmond, Virginia
Born: February 4, 1961, in St. Louis, Mo.
Married: June 11, 1988, to
Amy Elizabeth Kuhn
Born: August 10, 1964, in Oklahoma City, Ok.
German teacher
No children

ROSE MARIE - second marriage to DONALD EUGENE BRAUER, August 31, 1968, in St. Louis
                                 Organist and music teacher
                                 Born: March 23, 1933, in Minot, N. Dak.

PROF. ROBERT WALTER (brother)
Professor of music in St. Paul, Minn.
Born: May 27, 1933, in McNutt, Saskatchewan, Canada
Married: June 26, 1960 in Frankenlust, Michigan, to PHYLLIS PRUITT
                                                     Teacher and Real Estate Broker
                                                     Born: October 17, 1938

          Four children - One daughter and three sons
          Anna, John, Jeff and Jim (twins)

          John married Jennifer

ESTELLE ELIZABETH (sister)
Secretary
Born: January 10, 1937, in Indianapolis, Indiana
Married: October 10, 1956, to LARRY DOWNING
                               Minister of youth
                               Born: September 18, 1938

          Two children - Robert and Steven

                    Robert married Brenda
                         One Child - Amber Elizabeth

     9. ANDREW (dad's twin)
        Stillborn July 13, 1897

    10. MARIE MAGDALENE
        Born: 1900, in Boone, Iowa
        Died: 1915, and buried in Binford, N. Dak.
        (Died of Diabetes Mellitus at age 15)